SILVER LININGS

ISBN: 978-1-998315-34-5
         978-1-998315-33-8

Published by Inicio Press
iniciopress.com

Silver Linings

SILVER LININGS

ALYSIA TAORMINA

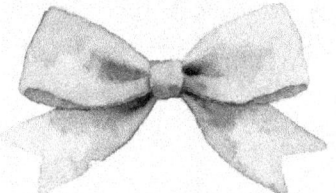

Dedication
to my daughters

To my first-born Paisley,

My angel in Heaven –

*Your life, though far too short, gave
mine a deeper purpose.*

*You showed me what it means to love
without limits, to fight even when it hurts,
and your spirit lives on in all that I do.*

*You are the quiet strength in my soul, my reason to
keep believing in light even through the darkest nights.*

To my little Jenevieve,

My light here on Earth –

*Your wild spirit, your fierce will, and fearless heart
have carried me through the hardest days. You
are my biggest reason to keep fighting, my daily
proof that joy can be loud, messy, and full of life.*

Because of you I am still here.

Together you saved me.

You are the heartbeat behind every word.

This book is for you –

My daughters, my miracles, my reasons.

Contents

Prologue

The truth is, you are not, nor have you ever been, in the driver's seat. It's easy to neglect prayer when all feels right in our lives. Maybe it's because some assume they are in "control." Perhaps it's because they think there is no need for a higher power. However, many are often mad at their version of a divine being when life takes a turn for the worse. Many also only pray when they feel helpless and in need. It's safe to say that humans are not perfect, nor is this world we live in. But it is essential to recognize that He is still with you, maybe even more so when life becomes challenging.

As Job says in the Christian Bible when his faith was tested, *"Should we accept only good things from the hand of God and never anything bad?"* (Job 2:10 NLT). When challenges arise, it's reasonable for anyone to question God's intentions or even His existence. I know I have. When the unimaginable happens to *you*, you may wonder: *Is there really a God? Why would He do this to me, a good person? Am I being punished?* These are all questions I have asked Him.

When I got diagnosed, I was not afraid of dying but rather living with a broken heart. Not only was I grieving the most detrimental loss a mom could endure, but I was quickly having to process the difficult changes to my identity and purpose here on Earth.

No one wants to live without purpose, importance, or meaning. I was convinced I had all of these, everything from an accomplished career to a loving family and deep friendships. I was wrong. "A bump in the road" was an understatement for what was to come and how it would impact our lives forever. As we grow and experience life, we learn to survive different levels of trauma. It takes time, but eventually, with patience, lots of work, and faith, you realize these experiences are blessings that carry silver linings and are, in fact, not happening *to* you but *for* you.

My story encompasses all the doubts and fears that come with any tragedy. I questioned God while having courage, strength, and faith to survive not just one but several trials, one after another. But I never gave up and am glad I didn't.

CHAPTER 1

Life Is Just Peachy

Faith is not immune to the storms of
life; it is an anchor that holds some
steady while others drift away.

Unknown

I never eat breakfast, but today, I was famished, so I decided to boil some eggs. While waiting for the water to heat, I walked to the guest bathroom around the corner to take a test. Yes, a pregnancy test. My husband Nick and I bought our beautiful new home in May of 2020 and started trying for a baby immediately. We had been together for eight years; we never thought we would get here. When we first met, Nick worked for an automotive service company while I was at a retail store selling health supplements. We were both making minimum wage. After four years of dating, we finally were at a place where we could tie the knot. By this time, I had graduated with a bachelor's in science. I then finished my teaching credential while Nick moved up quickly at a large automotive dealership. We both had blossoming careers and were ready to start a family in our new home.

We purchased our home on May 22, 2020, and began trying for a baby at the beginning of June. Throughout the month, I took about twelve tests before this one, all of which were negative. I knew taking tests within the month of trying was silly, but I was too excited. I assumed this test would also be negative, but to my surprise, there was a second line! I was pregnant!

After taking three more tests to confirm, I turned off the stove and called my obstetrician (OB) to make an appointment. At this point, my appetite magically vanished, and the eggs were thrown out. After this exciting news, I didn't know what to do with myself. I did not want to tell Nick over the phone, so I had to wait. It wasn't easy.

Since I had the time, I looked up cute ways to announce the news to him. I drove to a local store and went straight to the baby section. That part of the store felt so different when it was for me. I found some cute gender-neutral gray shoes, a onesie, a little blanket with an elephant head, and a hat. After I got home, I called Nick to get an idea of when he would be home.

"Hey babe, everything okay?" he answered with concern.

"Yep, sorry to bother you at work. I was just calling to see if you wanted pizza for dinner. Are you planning to work late tonight?"

"No, I should be home by six. Pizza always sounds good to me. Thanks, beautiful. Love you. See you soon."

I ordered the pizza that evening and asked for an extra box. I put a handwritten note inside it, along with all the little goodies I purchased and, of course, the positive pregnancy tests. I stuck the actual pizza in the oven so he could smell it. Nick came home hungry as usual and was ready to eat. When he opened the pizza box on the counter, he was confused. His eyes swelled, and tears ran clean lines down his dirt-and-oil-covered face. He was excited to become a father. We both felt incredibly blessed.

Many complained about 2020 being the worst year imaginable, but I was on cloud nine. While many of my colleagues found teaching from home discouraging and challenging, it was a win for me. I was so tired during my first and second trimesters, and teaching from home allowed me to rest rather than running around the classroom like a madwoman trying to keep track of thirty-eight-plus students. I could also make doctor appointments around my teaching schedule without needing a sub.

I was 5'2" and 108 pounds when I became pregnant. I lived an active and healthy lifestyle. I ate well and loved to jog in my free time. Once pregnant, Nick and I became protective of our health, especially mine. There was not a lot of information out there at the time regarding treating COVID-19 in pregnant women, so we did not take risks. Nick did the grocery shopping and ran all the other errands. I was always in the house and only left to get the mail or go for a jog. There was a lot of uncertainty about how COVID-19 vaccines would affect pregnant women, so I didn't want to take any chances by getting one. We did everything we could to protect our growing family.

Even though I was exhausted and nauseated most of the time, it didn't stop me from teaching. My mom had told me for many years that I was born to teach, and she was right. I loved every minute of it. I had only been teaching since 2019, so I was still in the "honeymoon phase" of this profession. In 2020, it broke my heart that I could not see my students on their first day of school due to COVID-19. It was hard for teachers and students, but we made it work. I grew to know them through the computer and got close to them with lots of time and effort.

During the summer before the 2020 school year began, I worked hard on the curriculum for my biology classes. I began having new intense back pain, which I thought might have started because I was sitting more than usual or as a result of my pregnancy. The pain was always there. Not only did it make it hard to sleep, but it also impaired my ability to do my job. It felt like someone was taking a scalding hot knife and stabbing it into my lower backside. I brushed it off as much as I could throughout the summer, as I had a new house to tend to and a curriculum to build. Unfortunately, the pain was unbearable by mid-August. I did everything in my power to alleviate some of the pain. What was once just back pain traveled down my left leg, and no matter what I did, the pain was there. I took Tylenol. Nothing. I stretched in the shower. Nothing. I took baths, walked during the day, and used a standing desk and a heating pad. I still could not shake the pain. This soon dramatically impacted my quality of life. It was worse at night. I went from eight to two hours of sleep almost overnight. *Boy, are pregnancies challenging,* I thought.

My husband and I prayed every night. We started doing this long before the new home, but we made it an even bigger priority once we moved in. We never missed a night of prayer. Our prayers evolved quickly with all the changes. We had new gratitude for our healthy baby growing inside me and requested healing for my back pain. With the COVID-19 scare, we were thankful for each day God kept us safe. Regarding my pain, we believed things would get better.

I fell asleep on the living room floor for the third time in one week. The last thing I wanted was to keep Nick up while I tossed and turned, so I usually would attempt to sleep in another room. I felt like Goldilocks trying to find the most comfortable place in the house, anything from a dog bed to the couch to even the hardwood floor. It was September, and the pain kept me from getting any sleep. My husband was worried. I was still teaching from home but felt like I was slipping because I was behind on grading. I was also slapping the curriculum together at the last minute and was not completing all assigned tasks for the biology department. Anyone who knew me knew that this was far from my norm.

The next night, the pain was still there. I was in tears and didn't know if I could carry the baby for six more months. I was leaning over the edge of the bed in pure agony, telling Nick, "I can't do this again; this will be the only baby we ever have if my pregnancies are like this." Without hesitation or an opportunity to argue, my husband asked me to get my shoes on. We were going to the emergency department (ED). He knew well enough that I never complain unless it's bad. He also knew that I hated emergency rooms. Unfortunately, emergency rooms at many hospitals are known for getting patients in and out as quickly as possible while often overlooking an individual's essential health aspects. Since I was pregnant, there were no ways to scan me safely and see what exactly was going on. The doctor I ended up seeing seemed confident that because part of the pain was due to pressure on the sciatic nerve, it must be related to the pregnancy. It was reassuring to know it was temporary, yet still incredibly frustrating. They gave me a safe dose of morphine that relieved the pain for thirty minutes. The nausea was worse, and the pain came back. It was going to be another long night.

Over time, my body became somewhat used to the lack of sleep but never to the pain. By the time summer was over, I alternated heat and ice all day while teaching remotely. I also used my adjustable desk, which allowed me to go from sitting to standing throughout the day to alleviate some of the pain. During the daytime, I felt better for some reason. I thought it might have been from the recent chiropractor visits or physical therapy. I did anything I could to get relief.

But the one thing that never improved was the pain at night. It came on hard and fast. It was miserable. I was convinced that I could not handle being pregnant again.

Fast forward to December thirtieth of that insane year. My belly was growing, and I still had terrible back pain. One night, Nick and I lay down after having burgers for dinner. I went to bed feeling slightly more tired than usual and had weird stomach grumblings. I didn't think much of it, as not many foods sat well with me at that stage of the pregnancy.

The next day, I woke up to a text from my good friend Bri, who lived down the street and wanted to go for a walk. I was anxious to go, as my stomach felt funny from the previous night. I enjoyed walking with this mama and her little one, who was not yet a year old. As I played "peek-a-boo" with her little one, I daydreamed about getting to make these memories with my baby one day soon. I frequently picked her brain about pregnancy and parenthood on those walks. As we got moving, the feelings in my stomach got more uncomfortable. I asked her about Braxton Hicks (false labor) contractions, as I thought I might have been having them. It felt like cramps, but I wasn't sure exactly what kind of cramps they were. She had not had these false labor signals during her pregnancy, so we were unsure as to whether I was having them. Not long after this conversation started, I cut the walk short because I didn't feel well. We both agreed that I was in desperate need of a bath.

As soon as I walked in the door, I ran myself a bath. The heat around my belly soothed me as I settled into the tub. I then dialed my doctor, set the phone to speaker, and propped the phone up near the tub, anxiously waiting for him to pick up.

"Dr. Watson's office."

"Hi, Dr. Watson, It's Alysia Taormina. How are you?"

"I'm well, how have you been? How's the back pain?"

"It's still there. However, that's actually not what I'm calling about today. Since last night, I've been having stomach pain that feels crampy, and it seems to come and go frequently."

"Since you're only thirty weeks along, the cramping is more than likely Braxton Hicks. However, being that the contractions have been consistent for this long, I would like for you to go to the hospital just to be sure."

"Okay, I will do that. Thank you so much."

I was annoyed, as I didn't feel like driving anywhere. *So much for my leisurely bath*, I thought. As I drained the tub, I carefully pulled my aching body upright, dried off, and dialed my mom to give her the update. While waiting for her to answer, I put on some comfortable clothes. I was dreading the long drive. As I waited, I counted between each cramp.

"One Mississippi, two Mississippi...."

There were about fifteen seconds between the first two contractions and exactly fifteen seconds between the next two. As a first-time mom, I was totally oblivious to the crucial timing of the contraction intervals.

My mom and stepdad happened to be out running errands not far from my house when she answered. I tried to downplay my pain to avoid worrying her.

"Hi, sweetie, how are you?"

"Hey, I was just calling with a little update from my doctor. No need to worry, but I wanted to let you know that my OB advised me to go to the ER to be checked for what feels like contractions. To be on the safe side, I am going to a hospital with a NICU, which means I'll be driving to San Jose."

"Well, we are already out and about; why don't we just swing by and get you? You shouldn't be driving in pain anyway."

The stubborn streak in my family runs strong, but I didn't fight this one. As a mama-to-be, I knew I would want to be there for my child in this situation. While I truly did think I could drive myself, I quickly discovered on the way there that I would not have been able to. After about ten minutes into the drive, the cramps became overpowering and painful. The burger I had eaten the night before could not have *that* much power. These were not "food cramps." These were *contractions*! They increased faster and harder within minutes. The drive that was only an hour felt more like seven; I was white-knuckling the passenger door handle and sweating while my entire body tensed up. I had even forgotten about my back pain, and I was grateful my stepdad was able to distract me with conversation most of the way there.

As soon as we were checked into the hospital, my mom called my husband. After many attempts to slow what we found out were indeed real contractions, the nurse informed us that they could not be stopped. The ultrasound technician informed the nurses that she couldn't find the head. The baby's head was too far down and had already started to crown. I was so relieved when my husband walked through the doors. I was nervous and terrified. The doctors and nurses did not understand why the baby was coming so soon. My medical records verified that the baby and I were healthy. The doctors were puzzled. Sometimes, faith can explain these kinds of circumstances more than science.

It was time to deliver the baby about forty minutes after Nick arrived. Breathing heavily through a mask, I begged for an epidural, and the nurse politely chuckled and said, "Oh, it's too late for that, honey. This baby is coming *now*!"

She wasn't kidding. Our daughter made her debut after only seven minutes of pushing. Due to her premature size, she came out all at once and was literally caught in the air by the OB. We didn't know she was a girl until she was born. We were overjoyed to hear the loud and healthy lungs of our tiny but strong and mighty baby girl. I had all of five seconds to see and hear my daughter before she was taken away. There was nothing natural about this. I had so much anxiety. Most parents are blessed with the opportunity to bond with their new baby by warming them through skin-to-skin contact and often getting to breastfeed right after birth. Our daughter, unfortunately, was removed from our room, poked by needles, intubated, and then placed into an incubator that would sustain her life. Nevertheless, we were confident, as the nurses reassured us that thirty weeks was a promising gestational age for a preemie birth.

We named her Paisley Renee Taormina. It was a lovely name that my husband and I agreed on long before my pregnancy. She was so beautiful with her blonde hair and long, thick eyelashes. We were fortunate that we were allowed to visit her twenty-four seven. Nick had a week off but then went back to work. I was ordered to be off for six weeks for medical purposes, and I spent all day, every day, with her. Every morning, I packed a large cooler with many healthy snacks and nutritious meals my amazing mother had made. I had to consume a lot of calories with the amount of milk I was producing.

During my visits, I did several different things to fill my day. I pumped milk every two to four hours, except when I held her. I had a binder full of pages to read and sign with various tips and valuable information on caring for a premature baby at home. I ate and napped in the quiet room for parents only. It was a clean room with comfortable lounge chairs and a fair number of snacks that were up for grabs. While pumping in privacy is nice, I found that pumping next to Paisley resulted in me producing more milk. I was also encouraged to change Paisley's tiny diaper and rub lotion on dry parts of her adorable little body. I loved caring for her in every way I was allowed, but my favorite part was holding her. As any parent can relate, the skin-to-skin bonding with a newborn is pure magic. The feeling is indescribable. She would wrap her tiny little fingers around one of my big fingers and hold on tightly while making little sucking noises and happy whimpers. Baby cooing, I believe it's called. As I spoke to her with her head lying on my chest close to my heartbeat, I knew she knew I was her mama. I made sure to coordinate the times I held her with Nick's schedule, too, so Dad could talk to her outside her incubator. We soaked in every special moment we could with her. Life was good—until it wasn't.

On day nine of Paisley's life, we got the call no parent wanted. Paisley was ill and going downhill. On this day, I was not at the hospital as early as I usually would be, as I had a long night of no sleep with the back pain we had assumed would be relieved after giving birth. I was distraught, and in no position to drive, so my mom happily offered to get me up there as quickly as possible. On day eight of Paisley's life, the doctors had started her on a fortification that was supposed to help with gaining weight. They would add the cow-based formula to the milk I pumped for her to increase the extra calories. This caused her to become extremely sick. She was suffering from what is known as necrotizing enterocolitis (NEC). Premature babies often have underdeveloped intestines, putting them at risk for inflammation and infection from cow milk. It is rare but always a risk.

When I showed up, I was relieved that Nick had arrived and was already speaking with the doctor. After our conversation about her condition, her doctor seemed somewhat hopeful that it *could* get better but never said the word "would." As the day progressed, my husband and I watched our daughter's skin go from a healthy olive tone to the palest white we'd ever seen. There wasn't a moment that day when I wasn't crying. Our confidence had been shattered. Her cries were not a normal pitch. Her strong and forceful cries told us she was in pain and helpless, and my heart broke for her. She had bloody stools in her diaper. Usually, changing her diaper was a treat, something I looked forward to as a mom, and I was itching to *be a mom*. This was anything but a treat. It was a devastating and terrifying thing for a parent to go through. While listening to her painful cries, I did my best to advocate for her and her comfort, but there was only so much her delicate little body could handle. After we begged for someone to alleviate some of her pain, she was provided with a low dose of morphine. It got better for a few short hours. Then it got much worse.

You may have noticed that I have not mentioned God for some time. That is because I was not sure He was with us. I prayed but didn't feel His presence. *Where was he? Why was this happening?* My prayers during that time did not feel heard. She was dying. By 10 p.m., Paisley was surrounded by doctors. They were fighting to save her life as they performed CPR repeatedly. Nick and I held each other while praying and hoping that our God was with us as we cried harder than we had ever cried. Her heart rate would drop, then come back up for a second, then continue to drop lower and lower. A few minutes past 11 p.m. on January 9, 2021, she left us and was with God.

We were permitted to have family join us in a private room to hold her and mourn her death despite the COVID-19 restrictions. My mom, brother, and father-in-law held our beautiful girl for the first and last time. My mom was the first to join us, as she was the first person I called when Nick and I were traumatically watching Paisley fight for her life. I am grateful she didn't get a ticket driving up. Then I called my brother Kyle and asked him to stop by my house to bring an outfit for her. I had no reason to have clothes for her at the hospital since the incubators were heated, and the babies were usually in diapers. My father-in-law Steve joined us around midnight. While this was such a difficult moment for all of us, we were thankful to have one another. We held her and talked about how she looked like Nick and me in different ways. We saw how beautiful she was now that she didn't have tubes and equipment covering up her features. She had my hair but her daddy's eyelashes. She had both our body shapes: long legs with a shorter torso. She was just perfect. My brother took several memorable photos of her with Nick and me. He also took videos and joined me when I bathed her for the last time.

Kyle later used the photos from that night and those I sent him of her living to create a fantastic slideshow with *the* most perfect and meaningful song. We cried while watching it, but it was so special, as we were all together, including Paisley. I was thankful to have some of our family with us that day, but I'm sorry we didn't have more of them there to grieve with us and meet our beautiful Paisley in person.

I wailed as I mourned my daughter's death. My husband cried with me while we held each other. This pain, the pain of losing a child, was by far the worst pain we could have ever imagined. Our lives could not have gotten any worse. I didn't sleep for what seemed like days until my body finally just gave in. With time, we let God into our lives again. We wanted God to know how sorry we were for not trusting and pushing Him away. I knew God loved us and would want us to lean on Him during this time, so we did.

While we continued to grieve, I was distracted by my back pain. We were at it again. The pain kept me up all night. No medications were touching it. As soon as I lay down, the pain would become almost hot, and I was forced out of bed with ten-out-of-ten-level agony. My pacing around our rather large kitchen island at two in the morning became almost routine. Baths were often taken at all hours of the night, Icy Hot was desperately rolled on like sunscreen on a sunny day, and all stretches taught by the physical therapist were regularly executed. My husband begged me to see my neurologist, hoping that we could get more answers with possible scans, as I was no longer pregnant.

Due to my extreme pain, they were able to get me in that week. I had zero motivation to go, yet the pain was so bad that I fidgeted when sitting in the car. I would go back and forth from sitting appropriately to loosening my seatbelt to sit in a squatting frog position. The ride was only thirty minutes, but my back likely wouldn't have been able to stand for even a five-minute ride. After the doctor got me settled in the room, he began our visit with some routine questions and physical nerve tests. He also was curious as to whether anything had changed since the birth of my child. My eyes started watering. I had not spoken to anyone outside of my immediate family about Paisley's passing.

"She's no long—"

I broke down; I couldn't even finish my sentence. Luckily, he empathized and listened with a caring heart. After I got past the difficult part of that conversation, I explained that the pain was the same as it was when I was pregnant.

"Okay, well, I am a little concerned, as some time has passed since you gave birth, and the pain is still with you. I'd like to do some scans on you, starting with an MRI."

The MRI was ordered that day across the hall in the same building. This was good because it meant that I would get the news sooner, and we could hopefully put an end to the pain. While I was waiting for my MRI scan, I browsed the internet for things that could cause this kind of pain that involves the sciatic nerve. There were many things, and I had no idea what mine could be. All I knew was it probably wouldn't be bad. It couldn't be. I assumed that I probably had one or two slipped discs, which I knew were painful but could be managed.

It had been over a week since the scan when my neurologist called. He began telling me that some parts of the scan needed further investigation. The tone of the conversation changed rather unexpectedly as I received unanticipated MRI results.

CHAPTER 2

Being in the 2 Percent

I can be changed by what happens to
me. But I refuse to be reduced by it.

Maya Angelou.

My upbringing taught me not to jump to the worst-case scenarios or overreact when given uncertain news. Worrying won't change anything, and we had no reason to worry. In my experience, most physicians keep a neutral tone when delivering any news regarding one's health. This neurologist, however, had a tone I will never forget. He sounded incredibly discouraged.

"So, unfortunately, I don't have the best news. The images show a mass on your spine's lower left sacral region. I'm really sorry."

Me being me, I felt like I needed to comfort *him* as I felt his sadness through the phone.

"Well, at least we found what is causing the pain," I said. "I'm sure we will have a resolution soon. I'm not worried. I'm relieved there is something that can be fixed. I'm grateful you ordered the scan."

I was at my mom's house when the call came in, as grieving the loss of my child was not something I wanted to do at home while Nick was at work. My mom had been working from home due to COVID-19, which was in our favor during this difficult time.

I ran into the house shaking a bit after the call; I wasn't sure how to react. My doctor's tone and referral to specialists had created an unavoidable pit in my stomach seconds after I hung up. I told my mom the news I had been given, and she and I immediately looked up possibilities for the mass. She started to name the findings Google spat out at us.

"Well, it could be a cyst, bone spurs, slipped discs."

The several Google results gave us peace of mind. The feeling in my stomach disappeared, and I was no longer concerned about the tone of my neurologist. I became eager to get this diagnosed and put it to rest. I was ready to be pain-free, at least physically, so I could get some real sleep soon.

The following week, I had a video call with an experienced oncologist. It is always scary, especially to those who love you, to hear that you will be speaking with a doctor who specializes in cancer. After meeting with this physician, I was confident we had nothing to worry about. He assured me that it was not likely cancer based on the shape and size, as well as the fact that tumors do not typically originate on the spine. When cancer becomes metastatic, it will often go to the spine, but it will have already originated somewhere else. This was a decent-sized mass resting in the lower left part of my back. Again, I was sure this would be an easy fix.

Regardless of what kind of painful growth it was, it needed to come out. My pain at night was unbearable, and the doctors knew I needed my rest to improve quickly. To rule out the several possibilities of what this mass could be, a biopsy was ordered by a bone surgeon in the oncology department. Before I went under the knife, he scheduled an appointment with me to go over all the possibilities of what they might find. There were several likely possibilities, none related to the "C"-word, which gave me incredible confidence. All the possibilities were manageable, from a bone spur to different types of cysts. However, to be thorough, he wanted to be sure to mention what was extremely unlikely but still a possibility as well. He informed me of a *very* rare form of bone cancer that it could be but was highly unlikely. I wrote it down but didn't think much of it or even investigate what it was.

Everyone worries when a loved one is awaiting results from a biopsy. Worry stems from the anticipation of discovering what it is and knowing it is not supposed to be there. I was preoccupied with the loss of a child and eager to get pregnant again. Therefore, I really was not focused or concerned about the biopsy results. No one could replace Paisley, but I longed to have our dreams of raising a child come true. The day we found out we were pregnant, we fantasized about the potential memories we would make while raising such a blessing. I was eager to give us a chance again.

After Paisley passed, I made it a routine to go to my mom's house daily. It made her feel better to know I was okay, even if I was sobbing on her couch instead of mine. I was lost without my daughter, but I had to remember that my mom had watched her child lose a child, which was also a challenging experience. We all wanted the biopsy results to come in so we could move forward without having it hang over our heads. I wanted to get better physically so I could also return to classroom teaching and work on moving forward.

The results finally came in about ten days later. I received a call from the surgeon who performed the biopsy. I immediately pulled out a notepad to write down the details.

"Hi, can I speak with Alysia? This is Dr. Avedian."

"Hi, yes, this is her."

"Hi, do you have a minute? I have the biopsy results and would like to go over them with you."

I didn't put him on speaker, so I could clearly hear everything he had to say. He had a neutral tone. He wasn't rude or monotone, per se, but he had no emotion tied to the results.

"Sure, go ahead," I said with a pit in my stomach.

He began by apologizing that the results took as long as they did but began to explain why.

"What we found was actually extremely rare, okay? So rare that we asked for some special pathologists to confirm what we found before informing you. This mass was confirmed to be what is called *giant cell-rich osteosarcoma.*"

I wrote it down, but I knew what had just happened when I saw the word '*osteosarcoma.*' I tried to cover my notes because my mom was standing nearby. I knew the word *sarcoma* related to malignancy and that it meant we would get to know the cancer world, but I needed to know if they were concerned about whether it had spread by going metastatic. Only a PET scan could tell us this. This kind of scan only looks for active cancer cells, meaning you did not want your images to light up like a Christmas tree. Of course, this was mentioned as an immediate next step, along with meeting an oncologist for treatment. I didn't ask many questions, as I was afraid to say any of these devastating "cancer vocabulary" words with my mom nearby.

"Is it treatable?"

"Yes, but we need to act quickly, as the mass is rather large and could metastasize at any moment. I will schedule an appointment with the sarcoma oncology team, and you will discuss future steps with them."

"Okay, thank you so much, doctor."

My mom is the strongest woman I know, but I still felt I needed to protect her. The weirdest feeling came over me as the phone call with the surgeon ended. I had gone from grieving and using my mom's shoulder to cry on to immediately finding the inner strength that I needed to fight this upcoming battle. Choosing to console both my mom and husband was a blessing because I was distracted from my grief to a degree and determined to be strong for them.

The second I hung up, I looked at my mom, who was staring at me with swelling eyes. I can count on one hand how many times I have seen this amazing woman cry.

"I'm so sorry, Mom."

I immediately stood up, hugged her tightly, and let her cry on my shoulder. I didn't shed a tear. It was strange. The roles had reversed within seconds. My mind immediately started to scramble to find a way to tell Nick the news without causing him to fall apart completely. He had just lost a child, and now his wife was diagnosed with bone cancer. *Seriously? Is this really happening?*

I didn't want to tell him the news while he was at work, so I gathered my thoughts for the next few hours while waiting for him to get home. That night, he came to my mom's house for dinner.

"Hi baby, how are you? How was work?" I hugged him a little tighter than usual. I was so nervous to share this news. It was like telling someone you did something you're ashamed of when you didn't do anything wrong.

"I'm good. How are you? You okay? What's wrong?"

I'm a terrible liar, clearly, if he was already on to me.

"Well, I wanted to let you know that the biopsy results came back. We have a plan to treat the issue, so I don't want you to worry. I will be doing some more scans and treatments soon."

"Okay, but what did they find?"

"Well, it's a form of bone cancer, a very rare form, in a bizarre place. This is probably why the first oncologist assumed it was not cancer. But I don't want you to stress, as it's treatable, and we found it in time."

I made sure to deliver the news to him with reassurance that there were already treatments being planned and that they would begin immediately. I also comforted him by sharing that my oncology appointment with the osteosarcoma physician was in just a few days. He was in shock but seemed calmed by my 'confident' delivery.

I went to my oncology appointment alone. It always surprises people when I tell them this, perhaps because there is always this big dramatic scene in the movies with your partner, friend, or family member holding your hand as the doctors deliver the news and treatment to follow. While I don't think it is always that way regarding the drama and always having someone with you, the fog that kind of washes over you as they stun you with medical responsibilities and daunting expectations of what is to come—that part is real, and it's like in the movies. Thank goodness I could take notes because it was a lot. He went over everything from having a port installed to in-patient weekly chemo treatments to needing extensive surgeries if the chemo does its job.

"I'd like to start treatment as soon as possible," he said, "so we should schedule for the port to be installed this week in order to start treatment next week."

As a biology major, I know a bit about chemo's effects on the reproductive organs. I knew that having multiple types of chemo given to me in large quantities was going to affect my fertility.

I began to lose control of my tears, which inevitably swelled to the surface.

"Is it possible to start treatment a bit later? I don't know if it's in my chart, but we lost a child at the beginning of this year, and I know chemo affects fertility. I would like to try to do an egg retrieval before starting chemo."

"I'm so sorry for your loss. I do have to inform you, though, that the cancer could spread in this time if we wait, especially depending on how long the in vitro fertility [IVF] process takes."

"I understand the risks, but I need to have hope that babies can be a part of my future while fighting this battle."

"As long as you understand the risks, I would say we can put off treatment for another couple of weeks at most. This means your cycle needs to start soon."

Part of my identity had immediately made room for being a mom. I felt incomplete without a child and was determined to make sure that this ability was not wholly taken from us. I needed something to live for. Some may not understand this, and that's okay. I doubt I would have felt this way had I never experienced being a parent before the diagnosis.

To do IVF, you must work around your monthly cycle. If you have ever given birth, you know that the next menstrual cycle postpartum is always a mystery. I prayed my period would come sooner rather than later. To my surprise, it arrived two days after my oncology call. I immediately called the clinic, hoping I could be squeezed in. I only had one shot at this and didn't have another month to wait. The clinic was incredibly understanding and empathetic to my situation. They prioritized cancer patients and understood the urgency.

After they scanned my ovaries while I was menstruating, they saw that I was incredibly fertile. That was great news! Typically, women in their early thirties become less fertile, but all women vary, and there is no other way to know. I began the hormone treatments right away, which required me to give myself a variety of daily shots. It wasn't terrible, but it felt like I was growing a baby when it was just growing follicles or fluid-filled sacs carrying immature eggs.

After the follicles grew and matured over a couple of weeks, I was scheduled for their retrieval. Mature eggs were the only ones that would be kept, so we needed a couple of weeks to allow this to occur. Thirty-eight follicles were extracted, which was *amazing*. Of those, sixteen were developed enough to move on to the next phase, which meant they would be placed into a petri dish with my husband's sperm to create embryos. Now, you can pay more to have embryos made by the human hand, which would mean that the doctors would assist the sperm in penetrating the egg; however, we did it old school since my husband's sperm was perfectly healthy. Within the petri dish, ten embryos were successfully created. Of those ten embryos, only four were developed enough to save and freeze. I empathize with anyone who has had to learn about this by going through it. It is incredibly stressful! In case you are wondering why we froze embryos rather than just the eggs themselves, it was because we were told by the fertility specialists that sperm have a more difficult time penetrating the membrane of the eggs after they have been frozen.

From one egg retrieval, we achieved four good embryos. This was a blessing that I was so thankful I had advocated for. It's common not to get any success within one IVF cycle, so to have four embryos made and frozen had us over the moon with gratitude and hope. In the meantime, I had already had my chemo port placed just under the skin, below my right collarbone. Mine was what they called a dual port, meaning I could have two medications pumping into me at one time through this clever device. The port allowed the nurses direct access to my arteries for all medication. Many cancer patients have these because they are much more convenient and consistent than vein poking. They are not permanent, though, as there are risks to having one. For example, infection can become serious quickly, as this blood goes directly to the heart.

Having the port placed while I was still doing IVF made it all so real. I realized that I could go straight into chemo after this was done. My chemotherapy was in-patient, meaning I would stay for a week and go home for two. I honestly will say I don't view IVF the same way as some. Many women talk about how difficult it is, and while this is true, I felt it was nothing but a privilege. I was lucky I even got the chance before it was too late.

My first day was difficult because I was confused about where to go. I had to go to a building to have my port accessed, meaning they poked it so the nurses could immediately hook me up to an IV later. In my case, I had a dual port, so I was constantly poked twice. One building was for accessing the port, while the other was for checking in and being cared for in a chemo ward. Eventually, I got the hang of it.

Everything about the chemo floor was excellent. When you first walked through the double doors, the floors went from a cold hospital tile to a wood floor that immediately warmed the unit. Smiles were immediate, whether it was your first or fifth time being admitted. The nurses were so sweet and empathetic, and the rooms were comfortable. They always had a hospital bed and a reclining chair, as we were encouraged to get out of bed daily and sit. With COVID causing rules to change almost daily regarding visitation, I didn't get to have more than one person visiting at a time and only two who could visit at all. My mom would visit most of the day, and Nick would try to come later in the evening after work. These were long weeks for everyone. This hospital was an hour and a half from home with no traffic, so it was incredible that my mom and Nick visited as much as they did.

No one can describe entirely how chemotherapy is going to feel, especially when there are so many of these poisons out there, and every cocktail is unique to you and your cancer. The week in the hospital did not feel like much, as the drugs were still working their way through my system. It wasn't until the last day that I felt a little crummy.

You might be wondering about the nausea and circling the toilet part of my journey. The movies ensure this is always in one of the scenes with someone fighting their disease. Fortunately, the nurses gave me specific instructions about when to take my anti-nausea pills to stay ahead of it. I took it around the clock for the first four days at home, regardless of how my stomach felt. After that, I could cut the dose in half and take it as needed.

Within the first few days at home, I was warned I would feel my worst. Little did I know that this meant I would be tired, weak, and lightheaded. My hemoglobin was very low, which meant not as much oxygen was getting to the brain and heart. Sometimes, my husband would have to help me walk as little as a few yards from the kitchen to the couch. This was all so new for us, and we knew I was "supposed" to feel crappy. *Cheers to doing this for the next five months.*

I had long hair before my diagnosis, and my dear friend Erica, who had been doing my hair for years, cut it to a shorter length before my first treatment. I was warned I would lose my hair; honestly, it was the least of my worries. But if I could do it over, I would have shaved it before it could fall out. Within the week of my coming home from my first treatment, my hair began to come out in chunks. My first concerns were about clogging the vacuum and the shower drain until it actually started to happen. I won't lie; I got emotional, and I think it was because the chemo was starting to feel real. My mom came over and supported me while Nick shaved my head. He immediately began to shave his, too. No one fights alone.

While I was home between treatments, my mom spent the day at my house, even if I slept most of the time. Nick was back at work, which was hard for him. My mom's being with me gave him peace of mind. The symptoms that came from the toxicity running through my veins were often weird, random, and unique to my body and its response.

I developed severe tinnitus from one of the therapies that caused a constant, agitating ringing. Fortunately, I was switched from this one to another before my hearing was severely impaired. I still have tinnitus to this day, but there was no hearing loss from the drug. I knew chemotherapy was going to make me feel bad, but it was always hard to gauge how bad it was and when to go to hospital.

I was told to call the oncology department for all concerns, as my immune system and bone marrow were taking a beating. For those who don't know, bone marrow makes red and white blood cells. The standard warning was to be mindful of my temperature and reach out immediately if it spiked. You learn a lot about your body through this less-than-desirable journey.

I never spiked a fever, yet I went neutropenic once. This was after I had completed four of the six planned chemotherapy treatments. Neutropenia means the body doesn't have many neutrophils, which are imperative to keeping our immune system afloat and the body safe. The ED became familiar to us between treatments. This trip to the ED was taken because of severe abdominal pain. As I said before, when on chemo, you cannot ignore any pain or weird symptoms; any discomfort can be severe. They always draw blood before much else is done once in a room, and this was a good thing. To our surprise, the blood drawn revealed no neutrophils. Not even one was detected. This immediately had the doctors and nurses gown-up and put me in an isolation room where I was near no other patients. My husband gowned-up as well. The doctor explained that my body's vulnerable state was life-threatening, and we were wise not to ignore my symptoms. We had no idea that my body could not fight any internal enemies. The severity of this situation was also alarming, as it was during the COVID-19 pandemic.

I was placed on antibiotics as well as food bags and fluids. While you can do nothing to boost your white blood cell count to improve your immunity, I did improve my hemoglobin and red blood cell count through several blood transfusions. I was a mess and didn't know it. I was thankful to be admitted, as my body was also depleted of platelets, which were replenished with donated frozen plasma. After a couple of weeks of being on food bags and antibiotics, my blood finally showed enough neutrophils for me to go home. Our blood can tell us a lot, and in this case, the readings and my husband's push against my stubbornness to go to the hospital for my pain saved my life. Unfortunately, this was one of several unexpected hospital stays due to complications from the chemo.

While I was fairly preoccupied with either routine hospital stays for chemo or unexpected admissions for adverse reactions to these poisons, I still managed to make time to investigate ways to have another baby. During my chemotherapy journey, I began looking into surrogacy agencies. While I believed I would be able to carry a child in the future, I still felt the need to do this for Nick in case I did not live long enough to do so. Neither he nor my mom understood why I was eager to do this, but they let me fixate on it, as it was simply an idea at this point; nothing was happening, and money wasn't being spent. Most of the agencies I had contacted told me to email them or wanted a large chunk of money upfront to discuss and view potential available surrogate candidates. This had me somewhat discouraged, but I continued my research.

I made several efforts until I came across an agency where a kind lady named Theresa spoke with me and listened to my story. "Hi, thank you so much for showing an interest in our agency. I am happy to answer any of your questions. Would you mind sharing what brought you to us?"

She had compassion for my situation, and before I knew it, I was on a list that would pair me with a surrogate. The agency sent me profiles of potential surrogates, and I decided whether they were a good fit. There was a lot to consider besides age, lifestyle, support system, overall health, and any other things that would impact the health of our child growing inside them. My biggest priority was a genuine connection and opportunity for a relationship between the intended parents and the gestational carrier. This whole thing felt like online dating, except there was no "swipe left" or "swipe right," per se, and there was a lot more at stake. I was emotionally discouraged, as I was not finding a good fit.

If you are wondering, yes, I did consider friends or relatives who had volunteered to carry for us when I mentioned the idea. There were not many who stepped up. In fact, one friend offered to carry for us right away, but she did not qualify. A clean bill of health, including healthy past pregnancies, is required for one to carry a child through the IVF process. At this point, I had given up and told the agency that I needed a break from looking at potential candidates. My mom and husband were somewhat relieved, as they were concerned about where I would be physically post-surgeries. With love and compassion in their voices, they explained the importance of waiting to plan for another baby until I was on the other side of upcoming procedures so I could focus on recovery first. While I didn't want to hear their reasons for this decision, I listened anyway.

"Let's just wait to see where you are at with your health after your surgeries, sweetie. Who knows, you might need more time to heal than you think."

Although I knew my mom was coming from a good place, it still hurt.

My husband chimed in with similar feelings, which made it even harder for me to know what to feel about pursuing surrogacy. "I don't want you to put so much on yourself, babe. I hope you know we are saying this because we love you and just want you to know that you are our main priority."

Their worries were valid, and I understood them. Truth be told, I had become tired and discouraged with the surrogacy research anyway. I shifted my mindset to the present and mentally prepared for what would come.

Since everyone undergoing chemotherapy has their own experiences, there is no book on what to expect and how to respond accordingly. For me, chemo was a burden, not because of how I felt about it, but because it impinged on my time and efforts to grow my family. I got annoyed and cranky because just about every time I was home from chemo to rest for a couple of weeks and have a break from hospital life, something went wrong. I wound up back in those rooms where the sweet nurses took great care of me. While I was grateful, I was still upset because it was not my bed, and I was not getting the break I was so excited for and felt I had earned at the end of every dang treatment. I felt married to the hospital but knew it was not forever. I completed my last chemotherapy treatment in July 2021. I was given three months to build up my strength for future challenges. What these challenges would wind up being was as much of a surprise to the doctors as they were to us.

CHAPTER 3

Wedded to the Hospital: My Unofficial Spouse

Courage is not having the strength to go on; it is going on when you don't have the strength.

Theodore Roosevelt

T he hope when planning to go into surgery is always that the surgeons working on you have performed this operation before, or at least something similar. It should have come as no surprise that a rare cancer found in a rare location would call for a rare surgery. *Great.* I was fortunate to have four very skilled doctors work together to perform these uncommon, invasive surgeries. I was reassured that the surgery plans were well thought out and not necessarily new to them, but they were not routine procedures. While I had been told in detail what to expect, I still was not aware of how my body would feel afterward or in between. Knowing what to expect from something you've never experienced is nearly impossible.

The three months leading up to surgery were a dream. I had been off chemo, my strength was improving significantly, and I could enjoy more of my time with my family and friends without the fear of needing transfusions of any kind or going neutropenic. Of course, this meant that August and September flew by, and we were into October before we knew it.

October 18, 2021, was the day one of my three surgeries. Yes, I had multiple surgeries scheduled, all of which would be done in one week. The first surgery began with the doctors making a vertical incision centered down my abdomen to push all the vital organs to the right side of my body. This allowed the tumor to be clear and for all those imperative body parts to be protected. Once the tumor was isolated, the nerves it had engulfed were cut, including three of the five nerves that make up our more significant sciatic nerve. An ostomy bag was placed to help me defecate during the recovery time. The recovery after the three surgeries would require me to keep my body completely straight, which made this bag extremely helpful. For those with experience with bedrest post-surgery, you might be wondering why I wouldn't just use a bedpan. The surgeries to come would have one rather long incision on my backside from the start of my crack to the middle of my back, which would pose a risk of infection if I used a bedpan.

I was kept under anesthesia from day one to day two. The first surgery was long, close to twelve hours. Surprisingly, the second one went smoothly and took less time than the first. The plan during the second was to remove the bone tumor and all the bone it had been in contact with and place titanium hardware to provide spinal and sacral support. The bones removed consisted of most of the left side of my sacrum and a few spinal discs. Two vertical rods were placed that ran parallel to either side of the spine, as well as seven screws to hold these rods in place.

I was awake on October 20 with pain I could never have imagined. I had heard that bone damage of any kind was one of the most painful experiences. As I've said before, you can't really begin to understand what something will feel like unless you've felt it. The bone was removed and drilled through in numerous places, and the mind-blowing discomfort made my childbirth experience feel like a walk in the park. The ICU nurses and doctors did their best to make me comfortable with powerful narcotics. I eventually stopped chasing the pain, but then I became paranoid from drug-induced hallucinations. I vaguely remember calling my husband in a panic from the side effects.

"I'm stuck. I'm at the top of an elevator and upside down. I know this isn't real, but I can't see anything else. I'm so scared, babe."

"I'm almost there, sweetheart; just keep talking to me. Remember, it's just the meds, babe. I love you so much."

It wasn't long before Nick found me in what seemed like a very white and sterile room in the ICU.

"Hey, sweetheart. How are you doing?"

This was the first time he'd seen me since I went in for surgery. He shared what he had walked into, as it was a bit of a shock at first. I was on a special bed that pushed air through the bottom, keeping my body from having any pressure on it. This, though, made me look as if I was shaking and, of course, could scare anyone unaware. He initially thought I was seizing but learned I was okay once I responded to him clearly.

"I don't know what is real, and I'm scared. I can't do this. When will this stop?"

"Just focus on me, love, I'm right here. When you start seeing things that don't seem real, look at me and focus on my face and hand touching you."

I had been kept asleep between surgeries, and the water retention from the meds and lack of movement had me extremely puffy. I was told that my swelling and the fact that my eyes couldn't focus or even look in the same direction had me seeming like a different person.

Unfortunately, Nick and my mom had to leave eventually, and I was left alone with my hallucinations. By this time, I was tired and just wanted to sleep, but I was paranoid and so frightened. I never knew when a nurse was real or not, as I would see one, and then another, and then another, each with identical strides and shadows. It was confusing and disconcerting. I begged one of the nurses to stay with me, as I couldn't stop crying. Quickly, I became embarrassed when I heard them arguing in the hall about my request. I knew they were short-staffed, and the request was not a small one, but I was uneasy about my medication levels for what felt like an entire day.

After lots of patience and support from the fantastic nurses, my husband, and my mom throughout the time I was awake, I was due to go back under for the third and final surgery. By then, my ostomy bag had been placed, the tumor and its surroundings had been removed, supportive spinal hardware had been installed, and we were ready for what are known as "flaps." Flaps are healthy tissue that can be moved—or stretched, in my case—from one part of the body to another. This meant I would have some upper glute muscle on the left side pulled up and into the sacral area lacking bone. This was to ensure that the hardware would not, over time, protrude through the skin.

I am aware that these surgeries may be unfamiliar to most and difficult to identify with, but I am sure one can imagine that the pain was incredibly intense, to say the least. Sometime during or shortly after my last surgery, I experienced something strange. I don't know when it happened because it was a surreal experience that I didn't share with anyone until later. I was unsure whether it was the drugs or if I was actually having a spiritual moment. I remember opening my eyes to a fuzzy orange color that seemed to dissipate. In the middle, growing larger, was a white space that looked and felt like a place I had always known and longed for. It was a familiar and comfortable sight, and I felt there was company while there were no faces. I felt like I was being spoken to, with no words coming from any mouth. It was like I was in two places at once and wanted to go toward the image that seemed not part of Earth. This image that only grew larger and so very white but so warm and welcoming became more and more of a temptation. It felt like I had to make a weird choice: go forward toward the image, which I guess was in my mind, although it seemed real, or look left or right to the reality I was in and stay there.

I know some might say this was just the meds, which it could have been, but I am not going to rule out that it might have been God giving me a difficult choice. I made a conscious decision to stay. That moment felt like forever with the vivid imagery I had in front of me. I prayed for this. It was an incredibly selfish and insensitive prayer, but I was terrified to know what life without my daughter Paisley would look like. I didn't tell anyone about this experience, as I was convinced at the time it was probably the meds and I was simply hallucinating. I found out that evening, though, that my heart had failed during the operation, and they had to end the surgery early. The left side of my heart had failed due to the severe stress my body had been put under with three twelve-hour surgeries back to back. This cardiomyopathy recovered with time, but I will always wonder if the image I so vividly pictured was an opportunity to say goodbye to some and hello to others.

I've had many people tell me how strong I am due to my pain and endurance during those procedures. Strength is subjective. What I went through was physically painful, and since I lived through it, some assume that means I have strength. But as I said before, I wanted to die. I secretly hoped I wouldn't make it. This was not because I didn't love my family or feared how I would heal. I missed my daughter. So, when I was reminded by my loved ones that I was strong, it didn't resonate emotionally.

Through chemotherapy, I had a cloud over my head most days. I was hyper-focused on pushing through any discomfort to ease the worry of my family. I was still in that mindset during and after my surgeries. Like we often do in our careers, I needed to put my head down and grind. I needed to survive because I had work to do. Survival for me consisted of not just getting through the surgeries but thriving and overcoming all the new obstacles my body had to face. As far back as I can remember, I have pushed myself to give every task or challenge one hundred percent genuine effort. I was raised to believe that giving my absolute best is all I can do in every aspect of life, and no matter what the outcome, I can be proud of myself. I was determined, hopeful, and motivated to get better. I truly believed and still believe that you only lose if you quit.

To everyone's surprise, I walked *three days* after my surgeries were completed. I was told by several nurses that it was amazing and that this was a great start to my recovery. That motivated me to get stronger and keep going. It was not long before I was walking without any support, all while still carrying my catheter and dragging around my IV pole with several bags of medication. I called the pole my Christmas tree because it had so much dangling from it, like holiday trees with ornaments. While walking short distances up and down the hall was encouraged, I was still limited in movement. I was not allowed to bend, lift, or twist, which made getting out of bed rather interesting.

My body's limitations called for new ways of doing things. For example, I would do what the physical therapists called a "log roll" to get out of bed. My gymnast's mind said it was like doing a cartwheel out of bed. My feet came down simultaneously with my upper body, pushing me from a horizontal position to vertically standing. I also had an ostomy bag, which required a lot of learning. The advantage of this bag was that I didn't have to go anywhere to relieve my bowels. That was the *only* positive. I was humbled by this "stool catcher" as I realized that some people have these for the rest of their lives. It can become a norm with time, but it took me a while to get used to the new responsibilities this bag attached to my body required.

The physical therapists gave me bands tied to either side of my bed near my head to keep my body strong while on bed rest. I was already physically disciplined and mindful of how to care for my body with food and exercise, so I was incredibly grateful I could work out while healing my front and back.

I remained at the hospital for three weeks before being sent to rehab for another five. After the first week, I was no longer in ICU, and this is when my healing and strength improved. The surgeons were amazed at how well my wounds were healing. I had two twelve-inch incisions running vertically down my front and back. Surprisingly, I had *no* pain in the front. *None.* It was weird, but I figured that my body was dealing with enough agony from the bone drilling and plastic surgery flap reconstruction and couldn't add any more pain for me to focus on. This was a blessing. I healed well during this time and was mentally prepared to stay at another facility to rehabilitate my back and left leg.

As my time was coming to an end at the hospital, and I was readying myself for another five weeks away from home, I received some unfortunate news. The pathologists who analyzed my tumor and its surrounding cells to find out whether the surgeons got clear margins (removed every cancer cell from the area) informed us that the margins were questionable. The data provided to all was not clear enough for my oncologist or surgeons to devise plans. After much deliberation among the specialists, including the pathologists, oncologists, and surgeons, they concluded that the margins were not clear enough to give me the green light to recover with remission in mind. My oncologist told me that I would need to have proton radiation to ensure all questionable cells left behind would be killed off entirely.

My area has no proton radiation centers, so I would have to spend six to seven weeks in San Diego, about nine hours away from home. I was devastated by this news and couldn't imagine being away from home for even longer than I had already spent. I told my oncologist that I was not going to do the radiation, and he warned me that there was a one hundred percent chance of the cancer coming back if there were any active cancer cells left behind. Anger and frustration ran through my veins, so I dug deep and decided to do the right thing. I agreed to do the proton radiation, which was highly recommended. It's often so hard to do what is right in these scenarios, but I knew it would be worse if I declined radiation and the cancer came back. I would blame myself.

The rehab center was about two hours from home, so the fact that my mom and husband came to me almost daily was amazing. This facility did not have the best nurses or doctors, but the therapists were outstanding! I was there for both physical and occupational therapy, so I chose to focus on the goals for each. My stubborn streak didn't let me sulk; I knew I couldn't change my situation. I wanted to make the best of it, as I knew my healing would be best off with a strong mindset.

Every morning, an occupational therapist (OT) arrived and taught me to dress from head to toe without bending. Their place in recovery is to aid patients with the necessary assistance for gaining independence in their everyday tasks; for example, they make sure you can brush your teeth, shower, get dressed, and so on. With my "no bending" limitation, putting on socks and shoes took some practice. I had valuable tools to help me with many of these daily tasks. A neat contraption helped hold my sock open as I slipped my foot in. The shoes were a bit easier, as I was able to get them on with a simple shoehorn. The physical therapist (PT) took me to an area with various contraptions and helpful equipment for my recovery. Their role in my recovery was to help me regain my strength, balance, and flexibility to be safe and independent.

The S1, S2, and S3 sciatic nerves were wholly severed in my left leg, which meant there were a few things my left leg struggled to do post-surgery. For example, I could walk, but not without a severe gimp, which caused jarring that would not be great for my back long-term. I needed to fix my gait, or stride, as much as possible and see how much activation I could produce in the left calf. Throughout therapy, I improved my posture and movement while still struggling to activate the inner part of my left calf. My PT helped me count the small wins, as I knew nothing would miraculously change overnight. My outer calf improved and activated, compensating for areas that weren't and helping smooth my strides with time. I still cannot activate my inner calf of the left leg to this day, but it doesn't stop me. My left ankle grew to be as strong as the right. This was remarkable because the surgeons warned me that it was very likely I would have what is known as a "foot drop" post-surgery, which means that the left ankle would be unable to move at all due to the nerve severing. This was yet another blessing.

While I was doing my best to remain optimistic about my situation, I was still homesick. It was also during the holidays when it was no fun to be alone. Thanksgiving was approaching, and I could not be with my family. I told my mom and Nick not to worry about me. I wanted them to enjoy their day without traveling or missing out on one of the year's best meals. My mom, being who she is, decided to cook up *all* the food we would typically have ahead of time and brought some of it to my hospital room. She and my husband both made this day so special. They came prepared and brought everything from portable warmers for the food to small coolers to carry it in. It was a Thanksgiving I will never forget. My spirits were good, thanks to my people. If you haven't figured it out yet, my mom and husband are two of the strongest and most selfless people I've been blessed to have in my life.

I was due to go home from the rehab hospital about a week before Christmas and was scheduled to go to San Diego first thing in January. By the time I had completed five weeks of rehab, I could perform most of my PT and OT independently. I still had guidance, but I was at a point where it felt safe for me to go home. I could care for myself using the new OT techniques and execute many important PT exercises. I had been away from my family for eight weeks, including surgery and post-surgery time, and was not in the best mindset. I went from being motivated and determined to improve to deflated and discouraged as time passed. I begged my therapists to sign off on my progress, which would permit me to go home early. I knew six weeks versus five would not make a huge difference. They were sympathetic to my situation and happily gave me the green light. I was so grateful to have that extra week at home before the radiation started.

I had a couple of weeks to relax and continue to heal before switching gears and preparing for radiation. However, to make the radiation experience a bit easier, my surgeons agreed that the ostomy reversal should be done. This meant that my "relaxing" time around Christmas would be interrupted by yet another surgery. This surgery was a good thing, but I didn't realize what the recovery would be like. I figured the reversal would require a one-night stay in the hospital at most, which was so far from reality. I was incredibly sore after they reversed it. This surgery required an almost eight-inch incision down the abdomen and manipulation of the bowels. It was not a minor procedure like I had imagined. Ignorance may be bliss, but it doesn't change the reality. I felt all the pain in my abdomen this time, and it was not fun. This surgery took five days away from me being at home with my family. So much for my extra week "off." While I was grateful and the surgery was a success, I was so tired of hospitals.

Any honest nurse or doctor will tell you that the hospital is not the best place to heal. I felt less pain when I was home, and it was almost instantaneous. While I was blessed to have my physical healing improve as quickly as it did, the emotional healing was overdue as grief abruptly rose to the surface. It was December, and our baby girl Paisley would have been one on New Year's Eve. It also would have been her first Christmas. Celebratory ornaments that represented amazing family milestones triggered memories of heartbreak and trauma. The way it hit me was surreal. It was like someone immediately came and sat on my chest, making each breath a struggle. To some degree, I was thankful for the time to sit in those sad thoughts, as I had put grieving on the back burner for almost a year. I did not have the bandwidth to mourn while trying to survive the chemo, surgeries, and every challenge that came with them. I felt I was living in two worlds: the one where I was a "cancer girl" fighting like hell to survive, and the other was the mom who lost a child and yearned for the day her heart could go on, even though it would never fully heal.

For a short while, I let the grief set in: I felt the sadness, I prayed and cried simultaneously, and I made sure that I did not feel guilty for it. There is no way to heal if grief is continuously swept under the rug. While sadness was present, I knew that decorating for Christmas was important and would be healing while giving my husband and me some normalcy. We have always enjoyed extra lights and color all around our wonderful home during the holidays. Not only did the decorating bring happy and sad tears, but it also helped me change my perspective on the losses I struggled with.

I ordered a custom-made stocking for Miss Paisley Renee. It had angel wings on it and her name at the top. It was beautiful. I hung this on the wall I had put together in our family room. It fit perfectly among the floating shelves with some special memorabilia saved from the hospital NICU. Going through the ornaments was usually such an exciting time. I was always eager to see which one I was unwrapping from the protective tissue and what memories it would spark. The ornament reveal was more therapeutic and healing this time, but not always easy. Some were related to pregnancy, the first Christmas as parents, and the first Christmas for Paisley.

I didn't hang all of these, only the ones that made sense then. When I thought I had gotten through all the emotionally challenging decorations, I came across ornaments students had gotten me. Those hit hard as well because I was not teaching. Again, this is another identity struggle I needed to work through. I told myself it was only temporary, and I would be back in the classroom next August to begin the following school year. I had so much hope, and though some of the tree decor pulled on my heartstrings, I was grateful to have good memories tied to them. I focused on the positives and did my best to remain motivated and determined to have some of my life back, like being back in the classroom teaching those lively teenagers.

As I had limited time at home with my loved ones, I strove to have only positive thoughts to ensure this time was well spent and that I would be better prepared mentally for the next chapter of my healing. January 9th was the day Paisley had passed the year prior, and fortunately, I was home to spend that hard day with my husband. Proton radiation was scheduled to begin on January 11th, which meant my mom and I would start the long two months away from our hometown on the 10th. I hated leaving my husband for this extended period. Still, I knew I could leave him indefinitely if I didn't follow through with this last form of cancer-killing therapy.

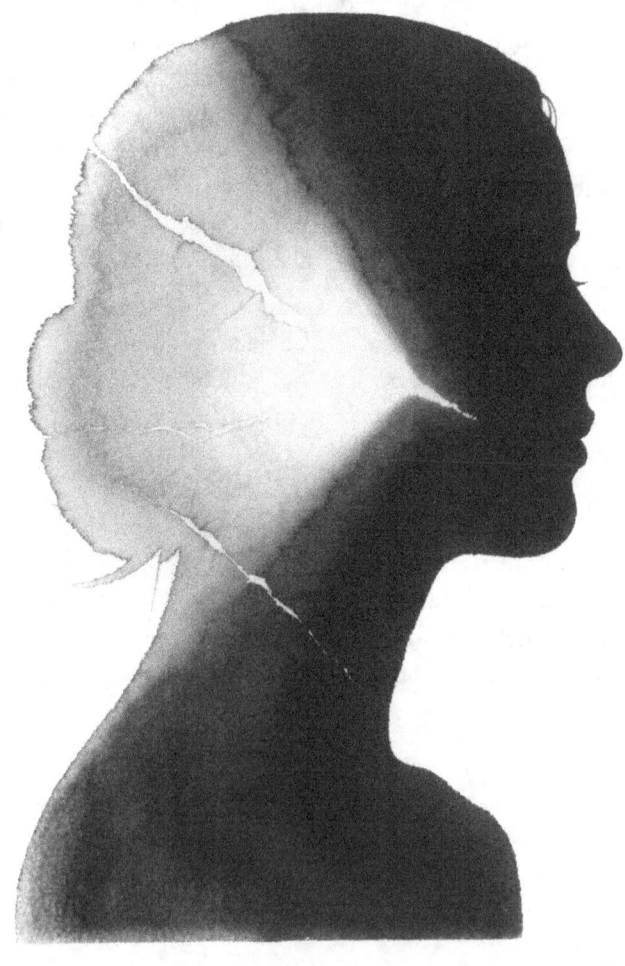

CHAPTER 4

Two Roads: Triumph and Trials Side by Side

He who has a why to live can
bear almost any how.

Friedrich Nietzsche

I had never gazed at a more beautiful sunset than those in San Diego. That was the first thing I remember my mom and me doing after settling into our seven-week rental in La Jolla. The beach was within walking distance, so these breathtaking views became our norm. I know it sounds cliché, but I really do think the ocean has healing power. While we knew we would eventually miss our husbands, we already longed for our fur babies. Luckily, dogs were everywhere. I would cross my fingers that at least one dog owner would let me say hello to their pup while strolling the beaches. I quickly realized this was not a bad place to be "stuck" for two months.

My proton radiation was five days a week and usually scheduled around eleven in the morning. My back had been healing nicely from the October surgeries. Still, the table I had to lie on during the procedures was hard, with only metal, plastic, and whatever they used to make the stiff molds for my legs. With very little fat on my back, I had close to no cushion to relieve me of the painful pressure caused by the screws placed in my back that would push against the unforgivably hard metal table. The leg molds were made to keep me still and in the same spot each time I received the radiation. Remaining still for this period was challenging, as the discomfort progressively worsened each minute.

I had not heard of proton radiation before needing it. The most common form of radiation against these illnesses is photon radiation, which can be done in several hospitals and cancer facilities. Proton radiation is not as common and uses a very different technology. I don't know much about how it's engineered. Still, the radiation I received was specific to one area, which was good. Proton radiation is more direct and precise, whereas photons cover a broader body area. Where I needed to be "zapped" was an area that had many vital organs within proximity. Because I was a young adult, the physicians were concerned about harming my insides and causing more issues in the long run if photon radiation was used. With proton radiation, the specialists can measure a specific window for the radiation to stay within, controlling the width and depth the molecules can reach to destroy any remaining cancer cells. I was relieved to know this technology existed but frustrated that I had to be so far from home to receive it.

I was grateful that the radiation treatment did not take up my whole day. Most days, it took about three hours. With no traffic, the facility was about twenty minutes away. My mom waited in the gorgeous lobby, which didn't feel like a medical waiting room. This place was aesthetically pleasing and had a warm, welcoming feel. Weird, I know, and maybe some who have been there would disagree. Perhaps I had such low expectations that I made it nearly impossible to feel disappointed.

In the first week, I met with the doctor in charge of creating the parameters for my radiation. He showed me visuals on his large screen that helped me understand what my insides looked like and where his target was. He did a great job explaining what was to be expected and his concerns.

"So, we will be targeting this area right here," he said as he pointed to the left sacral area where the tumor once had resided. "Now, we need to be careful, though, because if you look right here, that gray area is your small intestine, and we want to avoid hitting that at all costs, but this is a really tough spot."

"Oh, yes, I see it. Geez, it's awfully close to the area we are hitting. Can I ask what would happen if the intestines were hit with the radiation?"

"Well, it can thicken the walls of the smooth muscle they are made of and essentially kill that part of the intestine. It wouldn't be good, so we are going to make sure that doesn't happen."

I was at their mercy, so I tried not to stress about what was not in my control, which was essentially everything at this time. I did my best to be aware and stay ahead of the symptoms that could come with proton radiation. I was advised to put ointment and lotion on the affected area, as the skin often can become irritated and may peel or scab. I was warned that fatigue and some nausea were also common. With all I had experienced previously, none of this intimidated me. I simply wanted to make the most of this time and do whatever it took to get through it and be back home.

The week before settling in at the La Jolla beach home for two months, we made an enormous and potentially life-changing decision. I received a call from the surrogacy agency I had once worked closely with during my chemo journey in May 2021. The institution's coordinator called to inform me that a candidate had come on board with whom she felt I would connect well. While secretly hesitant and discouraged, I trusted her and scheduled a virtual appointment with the potential gestational carrier.

I was in my office doing volunteer curriculum building when the phone rang.

"Hi, Alysia? This is Theresa. We spoke months ago regarding your interest in a surrogate. How are you doing? How has your recovery been going?"

"Hi, Theresa. I am well, although I wound up needing radiation, so we are planning a two-month trip to San Diego very soon."

"Oh wow, Alysia, you have had quite the journey, but I am so glad your surgeries went as well as they did. I hope San Diego can be somewhat of a vacation for you as well. I am actually reaching out because I wanted to see if you were still interested in working with us to find you a potential surrogate. The reason I ask is because there is this one woman who I swear you would just click with. She reminds me of you in so many ways."

"Oh my gosh, really? I was under the impression that if I quit the process, I would essentially be placed at the bottom of the list."

"Normally, yes, that's correct, but this lady—Kristi is her name—is ready to call it quits, as she has not connected with any of the families she's interviewed with. What I like about her, though, is that she values the connection with the family she would work with, and I know that was important to you as well."

"Wow, I am actually speechless. I feel like this kind of fell into my lap as I went from surgeries and ICU stays to rehab for six weeks to now thinking about radiation. I really don't know how to feel, but it can't hurt to meet her and do the interview."

"I completely agree. I will set up the appointment here soon. Take care."

This Zoom session was scheduled for one night while I was in San Diego to have my molds made for the seven-week radiation journey that would begin the following week. Unfortunately, my husband Nick would not be present during the Zoom call as he stayed home to work. My mom was with me, which was great, as it is always nice to have a second set of ears when making big decisions like this.

This call could not have felt more natural and surreal at the same time. My heart knew this meeting was meant to happen. Getting to know a stranger and feeling immediate comfort, to the point of trusting them and their uterus with our embryo, was a feeling I will never forget. I honestly never thought I could get there with someone.

Before this scheduled meeting, I ensured that my laptop was charged and that it could connect to the hotel's Wi-Fi. I could have done this from my phone, but it is always nice to have a bigger screen, especially since the coordinator would be facilitating it and there would be multiple faces. While logged in and waiting in the Zoom waiting room, I tried to stay excited, even though my mom and I were both tired from the nine-plus-hour drive with LA traffic. I knew this meeting was a sort of interview as well, and this potential surrogate was already having trouble connecting with a couple of families they had met before us. This made me a bit nervous. *Would she like me? Would I like her?* I snapped out of these thoughts as I heard Theresa's voice come through the computer.

"Hi, Alysia; how are you? It's so nice to talk to you somewhat face to face. How are you feeling after your long drive?"

She knew our drive would be an all-day adventure, which is partially why the Zoom call had to be scheduled later. As I began speaking with her, I no longer felt doubt or uncertainty.

"Hi, Theresa, I am good. I am so grateful my mom was able to drive me down. It really saved my back. I want to thank you again for coordinating this and thinking of us after I took a break from surrogacy research during chemo."

From just one Zoom session, I could tell this potential surrogate was a strong, independent woman. I was anxious to see if we would mesh as Theresa had predicted.

I said, "Hi, Kristi, it is so nice to meet you. I am sorry it is so late where you are. Thank you for working with my schedule around my medical stuff."

"Hi, Alysia," Kristi said. "I heard amazing things from Theresa about you, and don't worry about the time; it's not that late for me. I have to tell you, after I didn't match with a couple of families, I was starting to feel like this wasn't meant for me. When Theresa shared your story with me, I bawled, and I don't do this. I don't cry easily—I can say maybe twice a year, and that's on my boys' birthdays."

While Theresa facilitated this call, it didn't need much guidance, as Kristi and I effortlessly began to bond.

"I will say that reading the profiles for potential surrogates became overwhelming for me while I was battling everything else," I told her. "It was a good distraction from a lot of it, though. I was hunting for someone who didn't *need* the money per se but was doing this to fill a piece of their heart if that makes any sense."

"It totally does, and I have to say that Ian, my husband, was not really on board after he saw me not click with some of the parents. He just looked at it as if it wasn't meant to be, and I began to feel the same. But after I was filled in on you and your '"why"' for needing a surrogate, I bawled my eyes out and told Ian that I *had* to do this for you. I just knew I had to."

Kristi was a fantastic choice for us, as she and I meshed well, and she had incredible support from a loving husband and two wonderful little boys. She assured me they were financially stable with established careers, which was essential to me. For me to trust someone to grow our baby through IVF, I needed to know that there was financial and emotional stability and support on their end. I also did not want the experience to feel like a business transaction. This woman and her supportive family would be giving the most precious gift anyone could give, which meant that I valued the importance of developing a forever relationship with them. Luckily, the potential surrogate Kristi's thoughts on carrying for us perfectly aligned with our priorities. After filling my husband in on how the conversation went, Nick and I agreed that this Zoom meeting was a success and believed that God brought this family into our lives for a reason. We said yes to moving forward with Kristi as our surrogate.

The benefit of beginning the journey with our surrogate was that it allowed me to have more hope for my future. While the radiation did exhaust me, my stubborn gene surfaced daily, and I refused to give in to the temptation of naps. My appointments were nice, as they gave us somewhat of a routine and got us out of the house at a reasonable time to enjoy the fantastic weather. It was pretty cold at home, about nine hours north of where we were for my treatments.

However, January and February in San Diego provided weather for shorts and T-shirts anytime. I was motivated daily to be outside, exploring the beauty around us. I don't know how I had the energy to embark on the last-minute adventures we pursued, but I'm sure God played a part in that. We did everything from hiking to beach exploring to zoo and safari trips, and three-mile walks to the frozen yogurt shop near our La Jolla rental.

Torrey Pines was a breathtaking location to both hike and walk the beach. We went there often after my morning appointments, as it was close to the facility and about thirty minutes from the rental home. We hiked a steep cliffside on our first visit. It was not an advisable trek for two ladies who had not been physically active outside of a year of hospital walks and bed rest exercises. Since this was not a planned stop, we did not know exactly what we were getting into. Sometimes spontaneity isn't the best thing, as we had no water for this treacherous hike.

Imagine a curved road that only goes up and to the right, making you feel like you will never see the end. I am confident it wasn't more than two miles one way; however, the constant uphill and down made for tired quads and weak knees. Luckily, the breeze was pretty intense, which kept us from overheating. Nevertheless, with flushed cheeks and wobbly legs, we survived and enjoyed the ocean view from a tall cliff. This was not the last time we visited this beach or hiked, but it was the last visit without water.

A week into my radiation sessions, I had unexpected and uncomfortable abdominal pain. The pain pulsated and intensified shortly after meals, even if they were small. Even when I chose to fast, I still felt discomfort. There were days I cried on the couch from the pain while sitting with my mom, who felt incredibly helpless. She would offer potential solutions, but none were solving my pain. Some days, I powered through the discomfort and did my best to enjoy the trips to the beach or any other fun destination we chose to explore in beautiful San Diego. I would often stretch my stomach wherever we went to the best of my abilities with rods and screws in my back, as it felt like something internally was pulling. Despite my abdominal agony, I never missed any of my morning radiation sessions. They never increased the pain anyway, so there was no advantage to skipping an appointment.

About two weeks into my treatment, my mom and I both decided that the constant pain should be addressed. The thought of continuing my stay for another month and a half with what seemed to be consistent soreness was discouraging. While I knew emergency rooms were chaotic, and I had often been to my fair share of them, the San Diego emergency room took the cake regarding organized hospital chaos. The sheer volume of people was mind-blowing. During this visit, we waited close to seven hours to be seen by a nurse and have my vitals taken. The wait was insane. We were packed in like sardines, and of course, this was not ideal for someone like me, with little to no immune system. But I didn't feel I had a choice. I was desperate. By the time I was seen, weirdly, the pain had improved, and I was unsure whether I would be taken seriously. Many people go into the ER for various reasons, but with my past, I *really* tried to avoid them at all costs. Finally, after about two additional hours of waiting in a semi-private room, separated from other patients by sheets and poles, a doctor saw me. The doctor was fair, as he listened to and acknowledged my explanation of my pain, but he did not dig deeper, as many in the ER don't. Nothing against them; I know they are pressed for time while trying to focus on whether something is serious enough for the patient to be admitted. If the consensus is not that the patient needs further attention, from my experience, the patient is sent home with a prescription or orders to follow up with their general practitioner, assuming they have one. This doctor did not prescribe anything but simply told me to try to avoid foods that are difficult to digest and to come back if the pain worsened. I was relieved to feel that there was nothing serious. Still, I was slightly hesitant to believe these results one hundred percent as I have had ER doctors miss life-threatening issues in the past.

For the next week, I tried to focus on the positives and doing activities that brought me joy. I love jogging as a form of therapy. I have done it for years, and I am convinced it makes me an easier person to deal with when my stress levels are high. While I would still fight the abdominal pain to some degree during this San Diego journey, I tried to tune it out with some good music and a morning jog alongside the beach before each proton radiation session. Our rental was just yards away from a beautiful sidewalk used for both walking and jogging with a view. I saw dogs everywhere, which was also therapeutic. I had mapped out a run that was a mile exactly one way, which was a routine jog or walk for me at least once a day. Not only did I do this for my mental health, but also for my physical well-being. After having an ostomy bag for two months during my post-surgical healing, my bowels did not work well, and the movement of waste throughout my intestines was still sluggish. Exercise had always helped me with that, even when my bowels were untouched, so this was not a new discovery for me.

It had been a little over a week since the last ER visit when the severe stomach pains crept in again. They were so bad that I was in tears, frustrated, and defeated. I would pace around the small rental, screaming internally with anxious uncertainty. The radiation was enough pain for me to endure, as I had very little fat. My rods and screws were pressed from my back onto a metal table daily for thirty to forty-five minutes with no cushion for relief. I did not need any more uncontrolled pain.

I was not feeling confident about going back to the hospital, as nothing was diagnosed the first time. Regardless of my discouragement, my mom and husband agreed that we needed to return. There was always a chance that something would be found or a new doctor would have a different and more effective approach. This time, my hopes were up because the pain was so bad I was sweating and shaking; I was sure something had to be found. While seeing so many humans packed into this small emergency room was still amazing, we were not surprised. This time, I ensured my mom packed food and water for her, assuming there would be a rather long wait. As expected, about six hours went by before we were seen.

At that time, however, the doctor tried something new. He was convinced that I could have an ulcer based on the pain I was describing. I was prescribed Protonix, which is commonly used for both stomach ulcers and severe acid indigestion. After explaining my recent history, the doctor felt I could have developed stomach ulcers from stress above anything else. I couldn't deny this, and Mom nodded the entire time he talked about how I had experienced stressful events in the last year and a half. We got home late but with more confidence, as we had a prescription and possible diagnosis. Luckily, this was a Friday. Therefore, my mom and I could sleep in without worrying about appointments. I prayed that the medication would provide the relief I needed—and fast. I was told it would take about a week to kick in. The pain increased with a full belly, so I was still cautious with my eating and made sure to drink plenty of water.

The San Diego Zoo was one of my favorite pastimes between radiation appointments. We knew the park's layout well after making the zoo a regular stop throughout our two-month stay. The zoo was the biggest one we had ever been to, so we hit different parts each time. One of my favorite animals there was the duck-billed platypus. I learned this egg-laying mammal was not found in many American zoos, so this sight was a privilege. The zoo was an incredible distraction, and I made it my mission to get a new stuffed animal (or two) with each visit. We won't talk about how much the stuffed animal collection added up to, but they were not cheap. They were for the jungle-themed nursery back home, which was chosen when I was pregnant with Paisley. I was confident that another baby would be there soon to enjoy these special plush companions—if not through surrogacy, through a miracle pregnancy. We *would* have another baby. I prayed hard for it and felt that it was going to happen. For the first time in a long time, I had genuine hope and confidence in something amazing for our future. I cannot explain this feeling in any way other than that I felt deeply that a higher power was guiding me.

The surrogacy journey ran parallel with my cancer fight. Yet, it felt like they also crossed paths intermittently. The hope for another baby to love on to help heal my mama heart gave me the strength and purpose needed to keep battling my illness. You don't have to know what chemotherapy, surgeries, and radiation feel like to see that they can mentally and physically wipe a person out. That doesn't even include the energy drain from grieving the loss of a child. Surrogacy was exciting but still had its stressful moments. There is a lot of red tape when it comes to bringing a baby into this world through IVF with a gestational carrier.

The first steps involve lots of paperwork about everything from mental health, finances, and health and safety for all participants. There is a lot of risk with any pregnancy, so both the family members of the intended parents and the gestation carrier must be on the same page. Lawyers and therapists are involved for a short bit. We were in a good place once the mental health checks were completed, along with the binding contracts covering financials and health and safety precautions. The contracts can be stressful because weird concerns and questions must be discussed and put into writing. For example, there are scenarios such as what both parties would like to be done if the gestational carrier were to become unconscious and in need of severe medical intervention. However, the baby could still survive if she were on life support. Such an icky thought and hypothetical situation, but these are things that must be in writing before IVF implantation because, as Nick and I know better than some, anything is possible, good and bad.

While chipping away at the surrogacy paperwork in San Diego was an excellent distraction to an extent, it was much more enjoyable and exciting to do it from home. My mom and I were on the road back to the cooler weather at home, where our hubbies and pups patiently awaited us. It was a pleasant surprise to be informed by my radiation doctor that I would be finished a week earlier than expected. While this seemed like good news, the early completion was due to concern for potential damage if the radiation continued. I had many vital organs that were, unfortunately, very close to the area they were focused on.

Pure exhaustion overwhelmed me on our drive back, almost as if I had been storing it. I put my best foot forward when I saw that my family had put up "welcome home" decor before my mom and I arrived. Truthfully, I wanted to hit the pillow, but they all had given so much support from afar and missed us dearly, including our fur babies. It wasn't more than a couple weeks after Mom and I were settled back into somewhat of a routine back at home before Nick and I were to meet our potential surrogate and her husband in person.

Before getting too far into the contracts, Kristi and her husband Ian flew from Illinois to California not only to meet us but to do some of the necessary bloodwork needed to ensure the safety of the embryo during implantation. It felt like a blind date, as none of us had met in person, and we were about to have a sit-down dinner together.

"How was your flight?" I asked with the intension of breaking the ice for all four of us.

"I hope the car rental and finding your hotel were not too stressful. Sometimes, the Bay Area traffic can be exhausting."

I was so nervous and as excited as Nick, and I sat across from these two extraordinary people.

"Not at all; in fact, Ian and I are looking forward to this short break from the kiddos. We are excited to finally meet you both in person. How was San Diego? How are you feeling these days?" Kristi asked.

As expected and hoped for, we all hit it off. Kristi and I connected and chatted across the table as if we had been longtime friends. Nick and her husband Ian were two peas in a pod. Their conversation flowed as well as ours, which shocked me as my husband is usually a bit more reserved. I loved how comfortable we all were. This was so much more than asking someone to watch your kid for a date night; it was asking someone to help grow our family. God was so good in bringing these wonderful people into our lives.

We were on cloud nine when we left that dinner. Our next steps were to complete the contracts and follow up with medications to prep Kristi's uterus for implantation come August. Our lives finally looked up, and nothing could get in our way. However, that stomach pain, the discomfort that took me to the ER several times, never did go away with the prescription. Unfortunately, it turned out to be a more significant health concern than an ulcer.

CHAPTER 5

The Finish Line Illusion

It's not how many times you get
knocked down that counts, it's
how many times you get back up.

George A. Custer

April 2022 came fast, and we were all hopeful that my healing would continue on an upward trend. My PET, MRI, and CT scans all confirmed that I was in remission. I felt a huge weight lift, knowing that the pain and suffering I powered through was paying off. The chemo killed the cells, the surgeries removed the tumor, and the radiation attacked the area where any cancer cells left behind would be destroyed. Life was going well, minus the annoying stomach pains I continued to have. This was where we began understanding what "let go and let God" means.

I was out on disability from teaching until August 2022. The plan was for me to return to teaching that upcoming fall, which I was ecstatic about. It didn't take long to realize that teaching filled my soul. I know some go into teaching as their Plan B, but this was my Plan A. I went into this profession believing that I could make a difference. My goal was to be a teacher who would not make any of my students feel like just a number. This is a big goal when you have nearly 180 students in one year of teaching. The high school where I taught is big, especially for a small town. It is the same one I graduated from, and I was so grateful to be hired as an alum employee there. As a student, though, I felt like nothing more than a number in most of my classes. I did not feel I could confide in any of my teachers, and I needed one to feel safe with. I went through a lot, as most teens do. Some students spend more time with their teachers in a week than with their parents or guardians, so it only makes sense that this adult figure could play an imperative role in their growth and development. I was excited to return to the classroom and wear several hats that many teachers should strive to wear.

My first year of teaching outside of subbing was in 2019. I was an intern, as my credential courses were not yet completed. I was teaching 180 students while going to school full-time at night. Looking back, I still don't know how I did it. I am better with less time and tend to be more organized with this chaos. I had an hour's commute to the campus where I was getting my credential. It didn't seem to faze me. I was eating well, working out at 4:30 a.m. every morning before teaching, grading papers, and prepping the curriculum after 10 p.m. when I got home from college. These were the days when three hours of sleep was enough.

I was grinding and thriving, and I loved all of it. I was new at so much and often felt unprepared for the job. Being responsible for thirty-eight fourteen-year-olds at one time is intimidating. I wanted to pee my pants the first week, as I had a hunch they would smell my fear. I taught five biology classes with the same lessons and assessments. This meant that my first class was usually my guinea pig group, as there were always kinks to work out to better my lesson plan. For those who don't know, I believe most invested teachers never feel their lesson is perfect and can continually be fine-tuned. My first group of students was patient with me but never failed to give their teenage input. I became increasingly callused in response to the criticism and grew to appreciate it as the year progressed.

The classes were called blocks and split into two groups of three. Blocks one through three were taught together every other day, while the remaining three were taught on the days between. Not all blocks were the same, and each group had challenges. At the beginning of the school year, block three was my most challenging in many ways. I struggled with classroom management in general, but especially with that group. A combination of things made this group more challenging, including the time of day, who was in the class, and the weather.

I had a fair number of what are known as non-grads in this class. A non-grad student didn't technically graduate from middle school but was not held back. I found in my novice experience that those who fell into this unfortunate category sometimes lacked essential skills for learning new material but also felt neglected and embarrassed. Their acting out, bullying, or defiance were all signs that they needed more from me, but I wasn't sure how to give it. A couple of my blocks were rough, and I struggled to keep them respectful to one another and focused on learning. Luckily, I had professors to talk to about this at night who were a soundboard for me. I didn't always have the time to speak with my colleagues at the high school, so I relied on any experienced teacher I could confide in and grow from.

I took an idea learned in a night class to the classroom. I was tired of students bullying and being disrespectful in my third block. I knew they all had many things in common, so I took the opportunity to prove it in hopes that we could all come to a common ground, be good humans, and make Mrs. T's class a safe place to learn. I handed out blank index cards to each student and put a prompt on the board. They were asked to write about one struggle they are facing at home and one they are dealing with at school. All the cards remained anonymous. After gathering all of them, I shuffled them and passed them back out. The activity was risky; I doubted they would take the assignment seriously. After passing them out, I had each student read the card in front of them aloud. They raised their hands if they related to the shared adversities of their fellow peers. I shared mine from my teen years. I hoped this activity would bring them closer, and it did.

Throughout the first semester of teaching, each class learned how to be kind and work well with others, regardless of what group they might be a part of outside our biology class. I intended to create a safe place for all. With time and several trials and errors, we all figured it out together as a community. As I said before, teachers wear many hats. I learned quickly that teaching science was not all I was there to do. I will remind you that I was, and still am a novice teacher, so my outlook on these many responsibilities can seem unnecessary or unrealistic to some. However, I don't see myself taking on this role with any other outlook. I enjoy all that comes with this career choice.

It takes time to build rapport with students, and every teacher has their way of doing so. It took less than two weeks for me to realize that using other teachers' strategies for classroom management didn't work well for me. I had to be my authentic self. My colleagues warned me that the students might take advantage of me if they knew I was an inexperienced teacher. But I *was,* in fact, a new teacher, so I decided to let them know and be candid about who I was. I knew trust would be built only with an honest foundation, so that's what I did. I created the groundwork with one sincere brick at a time.

Teaching is one of the most challenging but rewarding career choices. While some might think teachers are done with their day at 3:30 p.m., that's certainly not the case, at least not for me and my novice experience. Grading, curriculum building, meetings and calls with administration and parents, printing and prepping activities or labs, and so much more come into play. Most of these responsibilities done after school frequently went into the wee hours of the night. I never was bothered or shied away from the challenges or late-night tasks. I was always excited to share lessons with my students, even though they sometimes were a flop. That's learning, though, even for a teacher.

One experience I didn't know I'd have was losing a student. She was a fourteen-year-old fighting bone cancer. She had long, curly brown hair and the sweetest smile. She was absent often, but I never made her feel she had to make up all the missed work. I reassured her mother that I would not fail her for medical emergencies, taking priority over freshman biology. I didn't feel my class would have to be remembered to become a productive member of society or succeed later in life. I simply wanted her to enjoy my class in the moment. Unfortunately, she passed away in November 2019. Little did I know that I, too, would be diagnosed with bone cancer within the next year or so. This was by far the most challenging part of my classroom learning, and there was nothing from my credential program that I could lean on for guidance. It is safe to say that I learned a lot in my first year of teaching.

In the summer of 2022, I prepared to return to the classroom that August. While I was beyond excited to be back on campus, I was still struggling with unmanageable pain. While I still had abdominal pain, a new discomfort began to take precedence. My lower back on the left side started hurting with and without movement. It progressed rather quickly, and by the end of July, I screamed any time I moved. I was taking muscle relaxers and Tylenol religiously, but it was not enough. This new agony began in the middle of June, and I prayed the discomfort would sort itself out in time. With my complications, I never knew whether my pain was considered an emergency or if it was something I needed to wrap my head around as a new post-surgical reality.

At this point, I did everything I could to avoid going to the hospital. I had not been home for long after radiation, yet I was in pain. This was frustrating, but I did my best to believe it was temporary. On July 15th, I was handicapped by my pain and needed help. My mom came over to assist, but I saw her concern and heard her fear as she observed my attempt to roll out of bed without screaming. I reassured her that it was most likely part of the healing process and that I would be okay. This was not the truth, though. I should have been improving, but I wasn't. After I was out of bed and dressed, we stopped in the hallway, where there was a large mirror. I lifted my shirt to see if my back had any swelling or discoloration we should be concerned about. My incision up the center of my back looked great, with no redness, bruising, or observable swelling. The lower left area that hurt had a new red ring.

I knew that had not been there the night before, as Nick checked my back every night for post-surgery concerns. Why was there a red ring, about three inches in diameter, over the area where my tumor once resided? We decided that it was a medical emergency and rushed up to the ED of the hospital that had performed my cancer procedures.

I was dancing in my chair in pain and felt like I was running a fever, but I wasn't. The wait in the ED was the typical hour or so, but it felt like forever. Once in an exam room, I still felt like we were doing just that: *waiting.* I was freezing, and there was no sign of a doctor for over an hour. Usually, I would try to converse with my mom, who was also patiently waiting in a rather hard chair against the wall, but I was so miserable that curling into a ball with three blankets was all I could bear to do.

Finally, a doctor greeted me. Based on the lengthy wait time and how fast he spoke when he entered the room, he was very busy. I'm sure he meant well, but still, I felt his mind was somewhere else when I began to describe the pain.

"It hurts right where my tumor was, and I can't get out of bed or even press it against anything without extreme pain. It also has a red ring that we just noticed this morning. I want you to know too that I am at a nine out of ten for pain, and it takes a lot for me to say that."

"Okay, well, let's take a look. It seems a bit red, but that could be from you resting against something, too."

I could not have internally rolled my eyes any harder at this comment. I was there for a pain that was severe even to the touch, yet I am being told that resting the painful part of my back against something could be the cause for the discoloration. As mentioned before, ED doctors are looking for life-threatening conditions, and clearly, this was not one in his eyes. They can sometimes overlook something critical if the scans don't reveal concerns. After explaining my pain, its location, and how long I had struggled with it, the doctor decided to have an MRI done. I was relieved and hoped the soft tissue scan would show something. It had to. The MRI was incredibly painful because the hard table was much less forgiving than my bed, which was still the site of a nightly battle for comfort. The results finally came in, and to our unfortunate surprise, nothing wrong or concerning was revealed by the MRI. You never really want something to be wrong, but when the pain is so bad you *know* something is not right, you pray for a scan to find it.

Without any concern revealed from the MRI, the doctor suggested that I reach out to pain management, as they would be the best resource when I was discharged. It was now dark out, and we had been there all day. I was furious, but while I waited for the discharge paperwork, I reached out to pain management. It turned out that their earliest available appointment was in September of that year. If I was in the ED, this meant my pain was terrible, and there was no way I could bear to wait two months for that consultation. When the doctor returned to begin discharge paperwork, I stopped him and demanded another scan.

"I'm sorry, but please, we need to do something, anything. I know something is wrong. This is not post-surgery pain, and it's only gotten worse with time, not better. Can we do another scan? A CT scan, maybe?"

I was sure there was something they were missing, but I'm not sure the doctor agreed.

"Well, the MRI was the best bet at finding something based on the type of pain you're describing, but if you insist on another scan, we can do a CT to reassure you before you go."

They performed the requested CT scan, giving us a better look at the hard and soft tissue together this time. All my rods and screws would be visible as well. I prayed something would be found, as I felt that I was not well at this time. I was nauseous and cold but still didn't have a temperature. Not long after the scan, I was informed that they were admitting me. This was a relief because I couldn't sleep at home, and at least they could manage my pain better here. It was late, and I was tired. I assumed that I was simply being kept for pain management due to my complaining and would go home the following morning. To my surprise, I was not admitted for pain but for something found in the CT scan. Just as the pain meds began to provide some relief and I began to drift off, I was woken up.

"Hi, Alysia? Sorry to wake you. I am the on-call doctor for the unit tonight. I just wanted to check in and inform you that you are nil per os (NPO) as of midnight, okay? Can I order you anything for your pain in the meantime?"

NPO is a Latin abbreviation still used in hospitals that simply means "nothing by mouth." I was confused as to why an NPO was ordered for me, as this is typically an order placed prior to a scheduled procedure.

"Hi, I think I am okay, pain-wise, for now. Can I ask why I am NPO? Is it because of the meds? Is something planned for tomorrow?"

"Umm, well, no, and yes. They didn't tell you why you were admitted? Sweetie, you have a broken rod."

"Seriously? What do you mean? Is it cracked or shattered? How did this happen?"

Before she could answer, I started to cry, but she didn't know that they were happy tears. I knew something was wrong and was relieved they found what I assumed could fix my pain. I reassured her I was not crying out of fear but of gratitude and relief that something was indeed found.

The CT scan revealed that one of my two rods running parallel to my spine had broken completely. The right rod had snapped in the middle of two screws. The craziest part was that I felt no pain in that area of my back.

I continued to advocate for help with my lower left back pain, as this was why I was there in the first place. Before my scheduled rod repair, the neurosurgery team saw me frequently and listened to my concerns. They performed more scans, including an ultrasound of this tender area. Nothing was found. What little confidence I had from being admitted quickly dissipated when I realized that this surgery might not fix the pain I initially came in with. My hope going into surgery to fix the rod was that there was some weird connection to the left side, and my pain would be gone, but there didn't seem to be a connection. I continued to pray for an answer that would come in the operating room.

It was now the 17th, and I was scheduled to have my broken rod replaced. This meant open back surgery, but it was more straightforward than the last few I had in October 2021—or so I thought. As they wheeled me in, I begged the neurosurgery resident to look at the lower left side.

"Is there any way at all that you can look at the lower left side while you are in there?"

While obvious tears were streaming from my face, it seemed he already knew how to answer this question.

"Unfortunately, we cannot deviate from the plans to fix your broken rod on the upper right side. We are not able to do any exploration with what the scans revealed. We've done everything possible to determine whether something is happening on the left side, and nothing alarming has shown."

I cried and prayed that God would relieve my pain. At this point, that was all I could do. I was so scared, not for the surgery, but for the pain not to be resolved by the operation.

Nick and my mom waited in the parking lot during my surgery. It was not more than an hour into the operation when they got an unexpected call from the neurosurgeon. My prayers had been answered, but not in the way any of us would have preferred. They had found something astonishing. This was repeated over and over while Nick and my mom listened to the surgeons explain findings on speakerphone. They informed Nick and my mom that after opening my back to replace the rod, they found another problem: my back's lower left part. My small intestine had attached itself to the lower left bones that comprised the remaining sacral area and spine. My intestines had torn, and stool was leaking through the muscular tissue. My spine and hardware were at risk for fatal infections, and I was going septic.

The surgeries performed in 2021 were complex and involved multiple doctors. Two of the three surgeons were working on me the night when the unexpected fistula was found. Before this, I never would have known what this was. In my case, a fistula was the adhering of my small intestine to my spine and the remaining sacrum in my lower back. The small intestine tore at some point, allowing stool to enter my body. I was going septic. My neurosurgeon needed another surgeon who could save the small intestines and do whatever was necessary to stop the stool leakage, which would save my life. At this point, my neurosurgeon had to call the on-call general surgeon to perform the soft tissue procedure on my intestines. Unfortunately, he was unfamiliar with my case, which was not simple. After some explanation was given as to what I had done in the past and what was now needed, my neurosurgeon decided that it would be best to try and get ahold of the general surgeon who worked on me back in 2021—nothing against the doctor on-call. The team who operated on me back in 2021 knew my body well, and the reality was that they were pressed for time.

My general oncology surgeon from past operations was called to come in, and he did. I learned much later that he was returning from a trip and had just exited the plane when he got the urgent call. He rushed in that night with no hesitation. It was a blessing because I needed a lot done. After they sewed me up on my backside, they quickly flipped me over to open the front. The general surgeon, the same doctor who had placed my ostomy bag previously, was again working with my digestive system. He pulled my entire small intestine out and investigated it all for infection. He wound up cutting a few feet out that had been infected from the fistula and were no longer functional. This was fine, as we typically have close to twenty feet of small intestine. He repaired the fistula completely and placed something I had hoped I would never have to experience again. He put in another ostomy bag for recovery purposes. Dang it! After the infection was cleaned to the best of their abilities, they sewed up my front and wheeled me to the ICU.

When I woke up, I was not a happy camper. I went into this surgery thinking I would only have my back worked on. Instead, I had several additional unexpected pains to endure. I had staples along my old abdominal scar. I eventually saw the ostomy bag placed slightly above my first bag's scar. I didn't expect this, and with confusion and disappointment, I cried. It was two in the morning, so I didn't have the opportunity to speak with my surgeons. The wonderful nurses answered many of my questions, though, and I felt well enough with the pain meds to go back to sleep until morning.

I was on several medications, three of which were heavy-duty antibiotics. While the surgeons did a fantastic job cleaning me up the night of my surgery, there was still infection running through my blood and around my spine. The aggressive antibiotic treatment was to prevent me from getting a spinal infection, which could lead to paralysis or severely affect my life in other ways. We wound up involving infectious disease in my case, which I knew was necessary. They specialized in checking for and addressing infections and attacking them from all angles. I was anxious the morning after surgery to speak with my surgeons about what they did and why.

The morning after, I was extremely sore, but not so much that I couldn't speak with my doctors. They explained that the fistula caused my small intestine to open and leak stool, putting my body at risk. They didn't fix the broken rod, as all the metal was infected and needed removal. They didn't remove anything that night because my body had not yet cleared the infection. I needed to be hit hard with the antibiotic cocktail before replacing *all* the hardware. My body needed a couple of weeks to heal from all the infections. This still doesn't explain why I had to have an ostomy bag placed. That was the harder pill to swallow.

In 2021, the bag was placed because I couldn't bend for eight weeks. That was so the "flaps" created from my gluteus muscles could heal. Those muscles are important because my hardware and open sacral area depended on them. During this emergency surgery, the flaps were undone. I was thankful that my plastic surgeon was a part of this operation. Little did I know he would have more news about my upcoming procedures.

Before the hardware was replaced, I needed the meds to kill off as much of the unwanted bacteria from the leak as possible. This is all they needed to do, right? Wrong. I met with the plastics team to review their plans for this go-around.

"How are you feeling? We really didn't expect to see this. I am so sorry we wound up having to do more than originally planned. However, we want to try to prevent this from happening again. So, we need to do a bit more with this next surgery scheduled in a little over a week from today."

I assumed this subsequent surgery would be simple: replace the hardware.

"I understand that we are going to replace the hardware. I know that much. Is there more?" I had a lump in my throat.

Since the fistula occurred when my small intestines slithered their way down into the sacral hole caused by the tumor removal, they wanted to prevent any organs from having the opportunity to go in that direction ever again. This meant that they needed to block the hole more permanently. I could hear it in his voice that he was doing his best to comfort me while explaining the rather invasive plans they had in mind for my next operation.

"Well, from the back side, yes, we will definitely have to replace the hardware since it all has been infected. From the front, though, we want to create a barrier to keep your intestines from sliding back into the sacral hole you have. I will go in from the front and use your abdominal muscles on the right side as a barrier and sort of sling to keep your intestines out of the lower back area."

I was thrown for a loop when trying to visualize and imagine how my body would operate after drastic changes were made to my abdomen. It had been a week or so, so I felt good enough to respond sarcastically to this rather daunting news.

"So basically, you all are going to let me heal for another week, build myself back up, and then knock me down again, but even harder?"

I had a smirk, so I am sure he knew I was half-joking but also not hiding how frustrating this was.

For those wondering, the hole *was* blocked during my 2021 procedures, but it was done with a temporary mesh. This dissolvable screen was meant to hold long enough for all my internal organs to settle after being moved around, which I'm confident it did, at least for a while. There was a slim chance that my small intestines could fall into the hole, of which the surgeons were fully aware. They had a plan for a permanent solution to fill this space. However, I wound up having an unexpected stress cardiomyopathy, causing half of my heart to fail. This forced the surgeons to end the procedure early, and they could not execute the original plan for a more permanent solution to fill this hole. Their only choice was to have faith that the mesh would do the trick long-term, as they did not want to open me up again. Thankfully, my heart had healed entirely within that month, allowing for the possibility of having these unexpected procedures safely performed in 2022.

After I was back in my room and able to process my conversation with my surgeon, I relayed the information to Nick. I explained the plan to take my right abdominal muscles, cut them at the top, and pull them down underneath all my organs. From my perspective, I created a visual for him: the abs would act like a sort of sling or hammock cradling my organs diagonally from attaching at the bottom right front to the lower left sacral area. This was fascinating yet concerning. We both wondered: *How would my core be after this? How was I going to be active?* The plastic surgeon reassured me that I would be okay and my body would adjust.

As we approached the two-week mark of healing from the fistula surgery, I felt anxious. I knew this next operation was going to be a big one. I was going to have my front cut open again for plastics to rearrange my right abdominal muscles and block my sacral cavity. Then, the neurosurgeon would flip me over to replace all the infected hardware, which included the broken rod. I had mentally prepared myself and was eager to complete this. It was a bummer to know that I was going to get knocked down just as I began to feel okay.

When I have an extensive surgery scheduled with three surgeons onboard, I work hard to be mentally prepared. The day came, and I was ready. My husband had taken the day off, and he and my mom were on standby. I had fasted overnight and was incredibly thirsty, so I wanted to get going. I just wanted this to all be over. Remember, too, that I was so tired of being away from home.

There was a problem. My surgery was pushed out. It turned out that, somehow, I was mistakenly placed on what they call a "standby" list. This meant I would be shuffled around based on unexpected emergencies that arrived at any given time. This was not okay and would not suffice, as my surgeons had worked their schedules around my procedure, which would be an all-day adventure. It was anticipated to be a twelve-hour procedure that needed to start in the morning, and the room would be occupied for the remainder of the day.

One would think that a mistake of this magnitude would be fixed within twenty-four hours. While this is usually a safe assumption, it was not true for me. Again, I was not scheduled correctly for a day my surgeons had all prepped for. I had fasted for an entire day before I was given the go-ahead at 6 p.m. to eat and drink until midnight. I'm not one to complain about fasting, but the mental gymnastics I had to do to accept my situation were nearly impossible. I felt like a prisoner, as I was on bed rest, unable to bend to any degree, which made eating a challenge, beyond parched from the pain meds, and told that they did not know when I would have my surgery. My husband was taking time off unpaid because he'd used all his vacation and PTO time to be there for my surgery, which kept being pushed out. It was incredibly frustrating, and I was not good company. I felt bad because my mom and husband took time to be with me. I couldn't put on a good face any longer, and I felt like I was going insane with how little control we had over my situation.

Finally, after days of torture, my amazing tribe stepped in. My small group of relatives, who had been incredibly supportive since day one of our mind-blowing journey, got in touch with patient relations. We discovered that the surgeons had little power over the operating room (OR) scheduling and were all for us advocating. They wanted to get this surgery done as soon as possible, too! After we complained, patient relations contacted the schedulers and explained our situation. It turned out that necessary decisions and actions could be made with enough consistent advocacy from more than just the suffering patient. It didn't happen overnight, but I was eventually properly scheduled for an OR room bright and early on August 10, 2022 (a week from the originally scheduled day). My surgeons were thankful, too, as they were eager to get me in and on my way to recovery as soon as possible.

On August 10th, I had an extensive surgery I never thought would be needed, or at least not that close to my previous surgeries. Due to the infection from the torn fistula involving my small intestines adhering to my sacrum, all the hardware needed to be replaced, not to mention the broken rod. Due to my small frame and the break in the rod, the surgeons agreed to replace the original titanium hardware with a more robust alloy metal that would also fit my petite body better. Molybdenum rhenium was the name of the new metal. The hope was that no new holes would need to be drilled, but there are no guarantees. The outcomes of my surgeries seemed to be becoming less and less predictable.

My back was not all that would be worked on during surgery. I was going to have a lot done from the front as well. The plastic surgeon would slice me down the same vertical scar that had been cut four times already at that point. This was so he could rearrange my right abdominal muscles and make a horizontal protective barrier that would lay beneath my intestines and prevent them from falling into the vacant sacral area again.

With this many surgeries in a short amount of time, I knew what to fear: the pain management coming out of surgery. I had always woken up from these procedures in excruciating pain and wound up chasing it with the pain meds. It was no one's fault because knowing where anyone will be with their tolerance when they wake up is nearly impossible. From this current surgery that involved both abdominal and spinal manipulation, I woke up in the middle of the night and was screaming for pain meds. The downside to waking at this time is that there are usually fewer pain management staff members working, which typically means it would take longer for relief. Waking from surgery with pain that made me scream inside made me the worst company, so I was glad my husband and mom were not there for this.

It took a day or two for pain management to find the right balance for me with the pain meds. It's always tricky; the way it was explained to me is that our bodies build a tolerance to the meds, yet we need them for relief. Just because we need more to feel the effect doesn't make it okay or safe. Three weeks earlier, in July, I had gone off the pain relief I had been on because I would have built up a tolerance to them, making it difficult for me to get comfortable after my August surgery. It was like I got hit by a bigger bus than I had three weeks prior. My entire back hardware had been replaced, and my abdomen had even more invasive rearranging. I was tired and sore but thankful that this would be behind us. I was beyond grateful and blessed that I was in a hospital with surgeons who knew my body well, and I trusted them with my life, literally. There was no cardiomyopathy this time, either, which was a plus.

Due to the plastic surgery in the front and back, I needed to stay on bed rest for twelve weeks. I did about three of those recovery weeks at the hospital where the surgery was performed. During this time, I would perfect my log roll out of bed, which was still familiar from my 2021 surgeries. I also spent time with physical therapists who gave me small basic exercises to help recover my strength. It took about a week for me to walk up and down the hall without a walker for assistance. It was week four when I requested to do the remainder of my assisted recovery at a rehab facility. Since I was not doing any physical therapy and needed to remain in bed while requiring heavy-duty IV antibiotics, I was sent to a different kind of recovery hospital than before.

This hospital had a unit known as a skilled nursing facility for patients who needed assistance for longer durations. I only required nurses for the IV antibiotics and general care. My ostomy bag needed emptying, which I know is not their favorite part of the job, but it's better than dealing with a bedpan. I was pretty low maintenance, in my opinion. I hated being a bother, so I rarely asked for anything. Thankfully, Mom and Nick visited frequently, which meant I had help with things like emptying my bag or changing a chuck (an absorbent pad you lay on) that got wet from urine.

This hospital was in a town close to the ocean and was typically very cool. I was relieved because the week I was admitted, there were record-breaking warm days in August. To my surprise, the room was hot—ninety-two degrees Fahrenheit, to be exact. The doctor who oversaw me and who I thought at the time would be supportive when I voiced my concerns seemed rather misogynistic. He talked down to my mom and me every time we spoke and treated us as if our expectations were foolish and that we were unaware of what my care should be like. We were not ignorant regarding general hospital concerns and expectations, and this physician consistently shut us down.

It was impossible to feel heard in that place. My concerns were never taken seriously, and it created some of the worst anxiety I had ever felt.

"It takes over an hour for a nurse to come when I push the call light, and I get anxious because my colostomy bag is full and needs emptying. Is this the norm, or was it just a busy night?" I asked the doctor with genuine concern.

I would be there for weeks, so I needed his reassurance that this was not a typical night.

The doctor asked me about a sport in a tone that implied he expected me to be clueless because I was a girl. "Do you know how baseball works?"

Before I could respond, he continued to explain his oh-so-powerful analogy. "There are the major leagues, the hospital where you had your surgeries, and then there is AAA, AA, and so on. Consider this facility AA, so your expectations may be slightly unrealistic."

My eyes widened, and I'm sure my face told him many things, yet I was still confused and concerned. He reiterated to me that what I had experienced was considered the norm here.

"Plan on waiting an hour anytime you need a nurse, and if you are taken care of sooner, that's a win! Give it here!" He raised his hand for a high-five at the end of his little spiel. *What the heck?* I was furious.

Night after night, I called my husband, crying. My colostomy bag was full of stool, I needed water, my IV was leaking, and it was midnight with a room that was well over ninety degrees Fahrenheit. Whenever I pushed the button for help, someone from the nurses' station immediately came in, turned it off, and said, "Someone will be right with you."

Since a nurse was physically in my room to turn off the call light, I didn't see why they couldn't help me either. *Why did I need to wait for someone else?*

"Well, can you help me since you're here?"

She said she would send someone to help empty the colostomy bag and get me some water. This was foreign to me, as my many hospital experiences before this were nothing like this. No matter who came in or what patients a nurse oversaw, they were happy to help anyone in need. *I was on bedrest!* I wasn't allowed to get out of bed independently or believe me; I would have been glad to get up and take care of my waste.

Nick called many nights to talk to the supervisor and get me the help I needed. I waited over two hours for help on a nightly basis. I was stressed and hot, sweating even. The irony is that I had a healing wound on my backside that had sweat dripping down it, and I had just recovered from a severe infection. I was advised to stay there for six weeks on bed rest with a unique sand bed and IV antibiotics distributed that couldn't be given at home. I went through many of these struggles daily and had anxiety every night, knowing the neglect that would come. I also had to remind them of when it was time to replace the IV needles and tubes distributing meds through my port. The port is a direct line to the heart, so naturally, there are strict requirements for keeping the area sanitary and safe from infection. My port had been accessed many times, so I knew the routine. When I watched a nurse in this facility pull the pieces out without changing her gloves, I already felt uneasy. There are critical protocols to keep all port-accessing materials sterile. I'm not a nurse, and I knew this. This lady did several things that eliminated this process's sterility. I had had it at this point.

My family was done with my suffering there, and we all agreed that I would be safer at home. I purchased a bed with all the bells and whistles that a hospital bed has just two weeks before this unexpected surgery. God works in mysterious ways, as we had no idea this bed would be my get-out-of-jail-free card. I called my plastic surgeon and begged him to give me the "okay" to complete my bed rest at home. My flaps that were worked with during this last operation, front and back, in addition to the rearranging of my right abdominal muscles, needed me to stay in bed for the entire three months post-surgery. I was a pro at logrolling, and our bed was adjustable, so fortunately, this could be done at home. I had to keep my body straight for three months. This surgeon, who had operated on me several times, trusted me and my ability to recover from home with my family's support and said he would give the facility the medical notes needed to free me from this joke of a recovery hospital.

I thought I was good to go now that my surgeons were on board, but there was another problem. I needed approval from the infectious disease physician. I was approved by them, so long as I could get an in-home nurse to give me my IV antibiotics daily. That was not an option. I tried to find one in my small town. After many phone calls and research for in-home IV medicine options, I realized that my only alternative was to go on oral antibiotics. While this typically is very doable for most infections, this one was much more serious and complicated. I was reminded several times that this infection could lead to paralysis or fatality if it came back and went deeper into my spine. We had to be rid of it, no exceptions. While IV antibiotics were ideal, the risks of staying at this rehab facility outweighed the IV antibiotic benefits. I felt it would be safer taking oral meds from home, where my ostomy bag would be tended to, I could hydrate more frequently, and I wouldn't be sweating in a bed that I was forced to lay in. After I spent what felt like a lifetime painting a picture of this ineffectual rehabilitation center for the infectious disease doctor, I was finally permitted to continue my recovery from home using oral meds.

Thank goodness I have family, including some in-laws, who were angry enough to come to my rescue and help me escape this confinement. My father-in-law and mom gladly drove up to help me. It should have been a no-brainer for me to be discharged with the agreement of all my doctors and specialists from the hospital that performed the surgeries. Sadly, the doctor in charge at this facility was using various tactics to prevent me from leaving.

"Hey, so I know you want to go home," he said. "However, you have an appointment with infectious disease tomorrow, and I can't authorize it if you leave today. Are you okay with discharging tomorrow after your appointment?"

I'm no dummy. I knew what he was trying to do.

"I'm sorry, but I don't understand. Why do I have to stay here, go in an ambulance to my appointment, and then return to be discharged? The infectious disease doctors are not associated with this facility."

I could tell by his demeanor that he was not thrilled with my push-back.

"All I can tell you is that I cannot give you a proper discharge without you going to this appointment while being admitted here."

The doctor walked away, flustered, right as my father-in-law stepped through the door. I explained the conversation I'd just had with the doctor to my father-in-law, whose fatherly instincts had him fuming. When a nurse came in to distribute meds, we told her we were leaving and needed to sign the against medical advice (AMA) forms.

This poor nurse obviously had no idea how to handle this, as she went to the doctor I had just had an unproductive conversation with. He never came to our room, but the nurse returned and repeated what he had previously said to me about leaving the next day. We explained that we were leaving and needed the forms. This felt like a game, as there was no logical reason to keep us, and even my doctors from my primary hospital were confused. Everyone had given us the green light except for the rehab, which didn't make a lot of sense to me since the surgeons had the most clout in deciding how and where I would recover.

Since none of his "grand ideas" had come close to persuading or scaring me into staying, I confidently left AMA. I had *never* done that before, so I initially felt a little uneasy. My gut told me this was right, though, and the pit quickly disappeared. Since Nick had used up all his PTO during my time in the ICU, I was grateful to have my father-in-law and mom step in to help me escape that nightmare and ease his stress, too.

That first night home in weeks felt terrific. Nick and my bonus dad, Todd, had taken apart the bed and raised it for me the day they found out I was coming home early.

Nick was able to get off work early and help Todd quickly get the bedroom ready for my recovery. I slept so well that night. Having the assurance that my ostomy bag would not leak, my bed would be clean, I would not be uncomfortably warm, and I would be surrounded by people who sincerely cared about me was absolute heaven.

The little embryo growing in my surrogate kept me going during this time. With these unexpected setbacks, our little miracle developing inside this incredibly selfless human was what had me smiling through the pain. I genuinely believe it was God's plan to have this happen during a time when I was so fragile and feeling so helpless. I had a reason to hold on. It sounds terrible to say this, as if I didn't have other reasons to live, but I was tired of fighting. Nothing personal; I loved and still love my family, but I was emotionally and physically tapped out. But God had other plans. I was going to be a mom. Again!

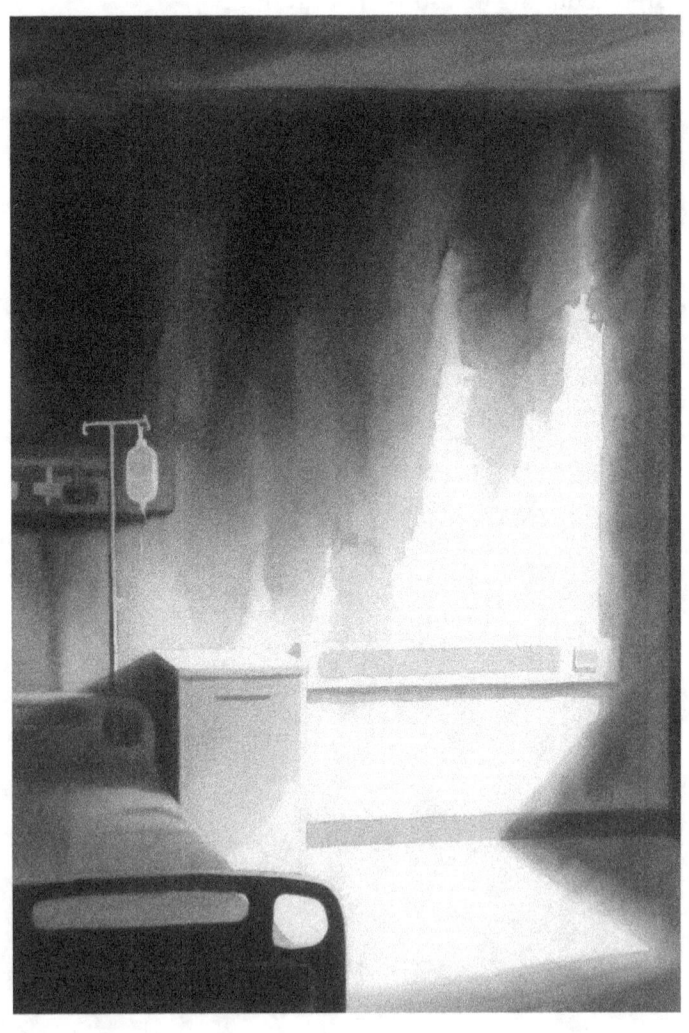

CHAPTER 6

Hospitals Are Draining

Health is the greatest gift,
contentment the greatest wealth,
faithfulness the best relationship.

Buddha

December 2022 arrived, and Nick and I could finally breathe. It is scary during the first trimester as miscarriages are more prone to happen during those first twelve weeks. However, babies growing through the IVF process increase the chance of loss even more than those conceived in the "nawtural" way. So many variables play into the IVF process that add risk. Just to name a couple, the injections that the gestational carrier gets have a vital role, as does the precision of the doctors at the fertility clinic doing the implantation. While a lot was on the line and the pressure our surrogate felt was incredibly high and unfair, she was a rockstar. She followed the guidelines for making her uterus hospitable to a T!

We made it through the first trimester and were much more at ease, but not completely. Paisley was born at thirty weeks gestation, so I knew I was going to stress until we were past that mark. I do not expect anyone else to understand it, yet I somewhat felt they would at least respect how we handled it. Seeing those who had compassion, even if they didn't understand, was eye-opening. To our surprise, not even some of my closest family members empathized, nor did they try to support our feelings.

Empathizing does not mean you have to fully understand what it is like to be in that person's shoes. It just means that you can sit in it with them and feel for them to an extent, despite not knowing entirely what they are going through. Sitting in struggles with someone is uncomfortable, so not all people, family included, are willing to do it, but it is a choice. It is a priority. It is a sacrifice to empathize, which means being there for someone else before worrying about your discomfort. If you are uncomfortable sitting in it with them, imagine how uncomfortable they are. The reality is that when life struggles come our way, those who are there to lift you up become your family. I know now that blood is not thicker than water.

That is my version of how we were and were not supported. Some thought we were selfish, as they assumed we didn't care about what others needed or where they were in their lives. They were not wrong in that we didn't invest a lot of time into the lives of others because we couldn't. I understand now that what was experienced can be defined as medical trauma. I don't throw the word *'trauma'* around lightly. For those wondering, someone who goes through medical trauma has been forced to experience the physiological and mental responses to something extremely challenging in the medical world. Prior to my cancer diagnosis, both my husband and I watched our daughter pass unexpectedly with medical equipment sounding, doctors frantically huddling around her, and scalpel incisions being made as last-ditch efforts to save her life. I can confidently say this is trauma. For over two years, I went through in-patient chemotherapy with many ER visits in between, had three twelve-hour surgeries back to back with heart complications, and then had to go to rehab for eight weeks. Next were seven weeks of proton radiation away from home with ER visits for unknown pain, which then led to me going septic and needing another two life-threatening twelve-hour surgeries. I am a giver and worry about people, but when going through all this and then some, I don't see how anyone had expectations of my husband or me. We were in survival mode and still are.

The surrogacy and surgeries overlapped. I believe the Lord knew what He was doing when He provided us with a surrogate and the growth of a miracle baby during this time. Kristi, the gestational carrier, was terrific. Not only would she send me texts almost daily about kicks and sensations of the little monster doing flips after she ate spaghetti, but she also mailed the pictures from each OBGYN appointment. When this process started, I knew I would be eager to learn as many details as possible. I didn't want to annoy Kristi, as she was also a mama of two and working full time. Fortunately, she must have known, as she was great at comforting me with daily and weekly detailed texts.

Kristi's husband and their two boys were incredible throughout these long months. Our journey began in January 2022 and wouldn't end until April 2023. Between paperwork, legal documents, medications, appointments, flight coordination, and the usual checkups for Kristi and the baby's health, it was a long process that took everyone's support to make it work.

Her sweet boys hugged and kissed their mama's growing belly goodnight. They loved this baby but knew it was not theirs. Kristi and her husband did a fantastic job explaining this complicated situation to two boys under the age of eight. The littlest one, who I believe was close to five then, would tell random people in the grocery store that this was not their baby.

"It's Nick and Aweesha's baby," he would explain. Then, of course, Kristi got to explain what the heck he meant by this.

Kristi was also great about staying healthy and doing modified workouts throughout this pregnancy. *Good for her.* I was not one of those overbearing parents who was going to tell her she couldn't have an active lifestyle. She knew what it took to keep the baby safe, and I knew she knew that. Her littlest, though, wanted to be sure. So, he would remind her by saying, "Mom, be careful; don't hurt Nick and Aweesha's baby" while she worked out in their basement. The best family was growing our kiddo, and we were beyond grateful.

January 2023 came rather quickly; it was now two years after Paisley's passing. I half expected it to be easier with time because that's what people (who have never lost a child) had told me. Speaking for us, it was not any easier the second year. Every year that passes, you are reminded of what milestones you *didn't* hit and what memories you *wish* you *could* be making. I hoped we could get through these tough days a little easier this year by focusing on the silver lining of our miracle coming in April. This, of course, would have been the case if we only had the surrogacy to focus on, which, unfortunately, we did not.

Nick had been sluggish and tired for months before January 2023. We chalked it up to all the stress he'd been under with my hospitalizations and work-related pressures. He had been diagnosed with GERD, or terrible acid reflux, months before this, and we assumed it must have been acting up again.

On January 2nd, I took him to the local hospital because he said his chest felt tight and his heart was fluttering. Chest complaints are more often than not taken very seriously, for which we are grateful. They got him in right away and did a CT, echocardiogram, and ultrasound of his chest and heart. The good news was that the ultrasound showed us the possible issue; the bad news was that there was no local cardiologist on staff at the time. The ER physician explained that it looked as if there was a lot of fluid surrounding his heart, and we needed to get him an appointment somewhere with a heart doctor soon. We immediately asked to be discharged and went to the oh-so-familiar hospital.

I took him to my usual hospital, which was much larger and had all the amenities, but it was further from home. Once we arrived, scans were repeated, and the fluid collection seen warranted immediate admission to the cardiac unit. He was in a lot of discomfort, and once hooked up to the monitors showing his heart rhythms, I realized that this was serious. He was tachycardic, as his heartbeat was at 160 while resting, and he was being monitored for it. The cardiologists had decided that they needed interventional radiology (IR) to drain the fluid they had seen around the heart in the pericardium. The pericardium is a sac that the heart sits in, and it is meant to hold a thin layer of fluid that can flush in and out through semipermeable pores. The amount of fluid assumed to be in there was far more than the norm, and his resting heart rate jumping spontaneously from seventy-five to 160 was disconcerting.

I anxiously waited for the IR team to come and take him. He was scheduled to be squeezed in as an emergency. Yes, it was an emergency, and I could not stand him having to wait any longer. When the cardiologist and his team came in on account of his heart rate bouncing dramatically while lying in a bed, they all stared at the monitors, almost seemingly in disbelief.

That was when the protective wife in me came out, and I said, "Are we going to just stand here and stare at him, or are we going to do something? He needs to be seen now! What strings can we pull to make this happen?" I used the politest passive-aggressive tone I could muster.

The doctor reassured me that he was going to make some calls ASAP, as his eyes showed obvious concern. The truth was that there was no available room to perform this procedure, but I argued that it needed to be done soon, even if that meant having the IR team come to his room. Fortunately, a room became available, and he was seen shortly after this tachycardic episode. I'd like to think my hospital advocacy experience was helpful in this unexpected endeavor.

While you might think that having the fluid drained would give him relief, he struggled even more as he had to learn to breathe with a painful drain tube shoved up his sternum and into his pericardium. I advocated for him as it was difficult for him to speak, and thankfully, with time and effort, he got the proper pain regimen and was able to rest. His recovery lasted a few days.

I stayed in a hotel close by for two reasons. First, the weather was dangerous for driving, and many roads were closed due to flooding. The second was more obvious. I was worried and wanted to be near him in case I got a concerning call. The day after the draining, we were given the results. They had drained 1.2 liters of bloody fluid from his heart sac. This amount was not something they ever saw, and they were shocked. The fluid built up when the pericardium became inflamed and could not flush through its pores. The callused walls allowed no fluid to escape. The blood findings were a concern, and we were told that it needed to be tested for cancer. *Seriously, what the heck?* We couldn't catch a freaking break.

I was stressed beyond belief, terrified, and staying alone in a hotel room, trying to be strong through this. My mom felt it through our conversations and drove up. I couldn't convince her otherwise, and once she was in bed next to me, I finally slept. Moms always know best, or at least mine does.

We were blessed that the cancer tests came back negative. The doctor said that the blood could have been from the stretching of the pericardium, breaking blood vessels over time. He confidently said that pericarditis (inflammation of the pericardium) started a long time ago. There is no way a pericardial effusion of that magnitude could have happened in less than six months. He was a healthy young thirty-year-old who had an active job and was somehow this sick. It really didn't add up. While there was no definitive answer to why this occurred, speculations regarding COVID-19 vaccines and their side effects were going around.

It was now a week—January 9th—and we hoped Nick could be discharged. While this was Paisley's day of passing, it was a day of gratitude because Nick was well enough to go home. I believed she was watching over us as our guardian angel then, making the day slightly easier.

Nick was incredibly resilient and strong after coming home. He stayed home from work for an additional two weeks, letting his heart rest while he acclimated to medication. It was a lot, and I was doing my best to support him in all possible ways. I was grateful his heart was beating the way it was supposed to. I realized that I could have lost him. That is how he must have felt during my numerous hospitalizations. We meant it when we vowed to stay together through sickness and health.

I had digestive issues that seemed worse than usual. I had difficulty urinating and defecating unless I was standing. Weird, I know, and probably TMI, but after so many operations, I was bound to have some complications in these areas. I chalked it up to the additional stress my family was enduring. Still, it quickly became a concern we couldn't ignore. The *last* thing I wanted to do was go to the hospital two weeks after Nick had gotten out. Of course, my fantastic husband and Mom convinced me to go. I am a complicated patient, and nine times out of ten, when I had been to the ER, I needed to be seen and was usually admitted.

I was annoyed but knew I needed help. I had been drinking milk of magnesia and taking laxatives, as well as using enemas and suppositories. None of them worked. After several surgeries, one can expect to adapt to new, permanent discomforts. This was different, and I needed relief. After a CT scan and ultrasound, the doctors discovered the problem. I had what was called a peritoneal inclusion cyst (PIC), which they believed developed from the reconstruction in my abdomen. The body doesn't like empty spaces, so naturally, it can form pockets of fluid within the empty areas surrounded by scar tissue. This cyst happened to be cutting off my lower bowels. We needed to drain it.

After several IR attempts to get to the cyst laparoscopically, they decided we needed to take another, more invasive approach. They had to open me back up, slicing down the same ten-inch vertical scar in the front from previous surgeries. It seems counterintuitive to perform another surgery when surgeries caused the PIC in the first place, but this was the last resort, so I was okay with it. I was desperate for relief.

The surgeon was the same one who performed the other surgeries involving my intestines, so I trusted him.

"So, my plan is to go in and clean up the tissue, drain the cyst, and seal it shut, hopefully permanently. I will do this by putting a couple of different irritants inside it. If all goes according to plan, the sides will adhere to each other, and there will be no room for fluid. I do have to warn you, though, it can come back, as these cysts sometimes do, okay?"

Hearing that I had to have this surgery to fix something that may return was not exactly encouraging, but what choice did I have?

"I understand; I guess all we can do is hope for the best, right? I need my bowels to work."

The surgery was successful, as they expected, but only time would tell whether the cyst would return. I went home three days after the surgery, sore as heck but eager to be away from the place that I felt somewhat married to. This would be the sixth time I had been opened in the front, from the top of my abdomen to my pelvic bone. It was amazing that the tissue would even close at this point. I was trying to recover quickly because we had a baby shower to prepare for.

We decided to have a small baby shower, even though Kristi wouldn't be there in person to show off the adorable bump. I had nothing to portray me as the mama-to-be visually. It would be different, and I knew it would be hard in some ways, but I also thought I would regret it if we didn't take this opportunity. This was not only about us but also a chance for our friends and family, who were over-the-moon happy for us, to participate in the ringing in of our little miracle. Most importantly, it was for my mom. I can't speak for all moms, but in my experience, most moms are jazzed to throw their daughters a baby shower. This was the most important reason for me to go through with the shower, as

I was a mom of a little girl in Heaven, and I began dreaming of making these kinds of memories with her minutes after she was born. It's what moms do. On top of that, my mom had not just been a mom for the last two years. She had been a caregiver, chauffeur, cook, housemaid, everything you could think of to help us. My mom deserved this and so much more.

While there was a lot to celebrate, I was still struggling around that time. I didn't know what triggers felt like before experiencing our trauma around loss. The reality was that I didn't just lose a child. I was also not getting to experience the pregnancy for the new little one. These triggers stemmed from losing the ability to carry and all that comes with being pregnant. I loved my pregnancy with Paisley, even with the chronic back pain, so I protected my fragile heart by setting some boundaries around these open wounds. It was nothing personal, and I clarified that to anyone who wasn't invited to the baby shower because they were pregnant. In the months leading up to this, I made known our feelings about our necessary boundaries with all close family and friends. We were simply just too fragile at this time, and frankly, still holding our breath, trying to enjoy our blessings while half expecting the other shoe to drop.

The baby shower was beyond anything I imagined. My mom always goes over and beyond, but this time, she outdid herself. She decided to take on not just one balloon arch but three. She was a brave soul. She decorated every inch of her house with such precision you'd have thought she had hired a professional. My bonus dad and his neighbor created some custom-made wood cutouts of California and Illinois to make it all come together.

Since the nursery was jungle-themed and gender-neutral, so was the shower. It was convenient, too, as the decor that could be used later would fit perfectly in the baby's room. My mom was efficient with her choices. For example, there were loads of collapsible storage bags and bins she had filled with toys and diapers at the shower that could later be reused to organize the nursery.

To make this day even more special, a fantastic local photographer, Mayra, who had heard our story, asked permission to photograph our shower before everyone arrived. I wasn't sure what those photos would look like or how I would feel about it all, but I had faith that it would be okay. I was thrilled that I agreed to let her work her magic that day. That special lady had two local beauticians volunteer to do my hair and makeup for the shower, and I felt so pretty. My day began full of gratitude. The pictures were taken creatively and gracefully on my parents' beautiful five-acre property. It was overcast, so the lighting could not have been more perfect for the morning session. We posed under a large pepper tree as old as me, next to the fencing that separated the horse pastures from the road leading to the barn. We also walked to the middle of the pasture, where the grass was as green as ever and even more so with the overcast skies. I wore a baby blue dress with a denim Levi's jacket and short Ugg boots. Nick wore a nice plaid flannel with jeans. We used ultrasound photos in most of the poses. We did everything from me holding them to Nick kissing me with one placed in his back pocket. The poses were so creative and unique, and she had a way of helping us forget that I didn't even have a baby bump for these photos. I also used my limited artistic abilities to make cute chalkboards for us to pose with. One said, "Our pea," and the other, "Her pod." It was our title for this journey from the beginning.

The turnout for the shower was unbelievable. Minus those who couldn't show up due to the dangers of driving

ALYSIA TAORMINA

on some icy roads, most came! We felt the love and joy. Even Kristi showed up over Zoom and talked to everyone as a group and even some individually. I'm sure she felt the love and excitement from all. My best friend from childhood and her mom, who was my babysitter for many years, flew out to be there. My aunt from Washington came, too. To say we felt loved would be an understatement. Our support overpowered us that day and washed away any discomfort or worry about the atypical shower. It was unique, and it was perfect. How many people get to say they've been to a baby shower for a baby being born via surrogacy?

CHAPTER 7

We're Not "Screwed,"
Are We?

It always seems impossible
until it's done.

Nelson Mandela

It was now March, and we took more breaths and felt more at ease with the baby officially reaching full-term. Kristi warned us that her babies like to stay for a long time, which eased our worries. She had a scheduled cesarean for the day she would reach thirty-nine weeks gestation. Having a scheduled c-section was easier for everyone, as there was a lot to coordinate, and the last thing we wanted was to miss the birth of our little miracle. Our baby was going to be born on April 5, 2023. We bought tickets to fly out the night before and planned to stay through Easter Sunday. Yes, this meant the baby would fly home at a week old, which isn't ideal, but trust me, we did our research before making this decision and felt comfortable. We didn't want to use up all of Nick's paternity leave in Illinois.

The weeks went by fast yet slowly. We were so excited to see the light at the end of the long dark tunnel we had been blindly finding our way through. The weeks began to fly when some unfortunate health concerns surfaced. We were partway into March when Nick experienced discomfort in his chest again, like the pain he felt in January with his pericardial effusion. He took no chances and drove himself to the ER straight from work. He made sure to go to the same one who treated him in January since they would have his history and cardiac physicians. We were so nervous, as the last scare was severe. If there was any good news to come from this unfortunate hospital visit, it was that we caught it in time.

He had another pericardial flare-up, but the fluid retention was minimal this time and was relieved with some anti-inflammatory steroids. Of course, we wanted to know the "why" behind this, as it had re-occurred not long after the first scare. The doctor suspected that the T-DAP vaccine we both got to prevent any chances of giving our baby whooping cough was most likely the culprit. There are many correlations between vaccines and inflammation of the pericardium, so this made sense to us. Since Nick had already had pericarditis once, we were warned that he may be more susceptible to these flare-ups in the future. We were reassured that we most likely found the cause, and the cardiologist suggested that if a vaccine is needed for any reason in the future, he should get on a short dose of steroids simultaneously as a preventive. While we do not take the consumption of those meds lightly, the pros outweigh the cons.

Nick stayed overnight and was thankfully discharged early the following day. While coordinating when I should leave our house to get him, he asked me how my back felt. He knew the car ride was a lot for me, especially when my back had been hurting for months. My back had bothered me since December 2022, but I started getting concerned and speaking up around February of the following year. I had been in contact with my surgeons, letting them know about my new level of discomfort.

Anyone with chronic pain knows that the baseline for their "normal" differs from those who are healthy. It makes it hard for me to know when I should reach out to my physicians, especially when my day-to-day pain has been so inconsistent and reset by unexpected surgeries.

Nick suggested that I get checked out and maybe get some better pain meds before flying and spending a week in Illinois.

"If you have this much pain now, love, imagine how you will be with a five-hour plane ride, long car rides, and a bed that probably won't be as comfortable as ours," he said. "You should at least go into the ER, so if nothing else, they prescribe some better pain meds until we get back, and you can see your regular doctors."

"But you need to be discharged. I can't discharge you while in the ED. Maybe my mom could come with me to help. I will go to the ED, and my mom will be there to pick you up when you are discharged."

"Your mom most likely isn't going to let you drive yourself anyway, not with the pain you're in. After I am discharged, she and I can come wait with you."

I was learning to deal with the pain and let it be the norm, but then, preparing to care for a little one, I realized that I needed my back in the best possible shape. I was not okay with the idea of taking care of the baby while having this kind of back discomfort. It was simply not tolerable.

My mom and I drove up, sitting in the usual traffic for an hour and a half, just to be in the ED for another two at least. I have the best mom. Nick and I were fortunate to be seen at the same hospital. We never bothered to go to our local hospitals at this point. We had our health scares diagnosed and treated at this facility, so it only made sense for us to continue to be seen here, even if it was a bit of a drive. There was no way to summarize my health history over the last year and a half, and it would be tough to catch doctors up at any other hospital. All three of us being in the same building meant my mom could be there for Nick's discharge, and she could sit with me in the meantime while they got to the bottom of why my pain had recently increased.

The norm for my visits is for the doctors to request a CT and MRI to get a complete picture of the hard and soft tissue. This time, though, they decided to add an x-ray. It was a standing one, which I don't usually do. I was grateful they wanted a complete picture, but I wasn't expecting the x-ray images to give them much more than they already had from the previous scans. It seemed silly to do one, but I was glad they did.

While waiting for the results, we simultaneously coordinated Nick's discharge from the cardiac unit. My mom would get him, and we would most likely head home together after completing my scans. Well, that was a short-lived hypothesis, as I was given shocking results from the scans that would have me on bed rest in the blink of an eye.

"Miss, we need you to remain in bed, and please hit the call light if you need to use the restroom," one of the nurses told me while we waited patiently for the doctor to return with the readings.

I was confused and asked why.

They explained that I had a broken screw and needed to be admitted for surgery. I was in disbelief and asked to see the films that showed that diagnosis. It wasn't long before the doctor explained what they had found.

The largest screw in my body, which was in the lower left sacral and pelvic area, had broken off at the head, putting the screw at a suboptimal angle. To provide a visual, two rods ran parallel on either side of the lower lumbar spine. On the right side, since there was no sacral bone missing, there were four screws spaced appropriately that drilled through both the rod and bones to hold everything in place. The left side was similar, except that the sacrum was nearly gone, so there was a larger screw running on the bottom and only three in total on this side. Unfortunately, this significant screw breaking was causing all the angles of the connecting metal to change and needed to be fixed.

I was not the most tolerant patient because I knew what day it was and how close we were to having our little miracle. Our baby was about to be born in a couple of weeks, so I instantly regretted the decision to go in—as if traveling with a broken screw would have been a better option. What we don't know won't hurt us, right? Well, not in this case. The ER doctor explained the severity of this broken hardware and that any wrong movement could impair the nerves surrounding it. It's unfortunate that our pelvis shifts with almost every body movement.

"Well, I have somewhere to be in two weeks, so I hope this can be taken care of ASAP," I said with make-believe authority.

People must advocate for themselves, especially in overpopulated hospitals like this one. Otherwise, they will do what is most convenient but not best for you.

Don't get me wrong, I usually am an accommodating patient to work with. I usually won't even ask for a blanket if the nurse doesn't already have one in their hand. I hate inconveniencing others, but dang it, I had waited too long and fought incredibly hard not to be there for the birth of our baby due to another setback. My neurosurgeon, who knew me well then, was excellent. They admitted me for surgery within the next day or two. I was grateful.

It's funny to look at the irony of our situation. By the time I was admitted, Nick was ready to be discharged from the cardiac unit. So, my mom left the ED and got in her car to pick Nick up from the front of the main hospital. They drove into the parking garage and headed up to the neuro unit, where I would stay. *What were the odds all of this would happen?*

I shook my head and said, "I just wanted them to give me something for the pain so I could travel. I wasn't expecting surgery out of this visit."

We had to laugh at how ridiculous the whole thing was, as it was barely March, and Nick had already had a severe pericardial effusion, I had PIC surgery in the front, and now more crap.

On the bright side, we were happy the surgery was happening before the baby was home. My surgeon knew what I had been through, so he was great about not giving me too many restrictions. I was afraid I would be told I couldn't fly, but a car would be so much harder on my back than a flight. He gave the okay for travel, but there was to be "no bending, lifting, or twisting." Of course, there were exceptions for holding the baby, given that they would most likely weigh more than five pounds, which was my lifting and carrying weight limit.

I was discharged two days post-surgery. Crazy, I know, but I was confident that I would heal faster from home. The surgery consisted of them re-opening my twelve-inch back incision, removing the broken screw in the lower left sacral area, and replacing it with a new but identical screw. I had a million things to do and prepare. Thankfully, I was already done packing for the baby and only needed to think about us. My clothing choices changed slightly after this procedure, as I was going to be traveling with a back full of stitches and some evident back inflammation. The stitches needed to be in for three weeks before being removed. I also had to make room for the large back brace, which I was convinced I would never have to pull out again. These are not hard things, but when planning for something as big as bringing a child into the world and you are hundreds of miles from home, you want the time and space to think and prepare without constant interruption every couple of hours from gracious nurses caring for you.

I loved nearly all my nurses. They took such incredible care of me. I had to be home, and they all understood and didn't take it personally when I begged to be discharged early. My surgeons all knew I needed to be out as well, and I was beyond thankful they understood. What a wild ride the whole first quarter of the year was! Thankfully, Kristi was okay. I was nervous to share our health hiccups with her. I wasn't afraid of judgment, but simply stressing her out and having her wonder whether we would be there for the birth. She knew how much we had fought for this and was rooting for us to have the experience we deserved. I assured her that we were not missing this. Next stop, baby!

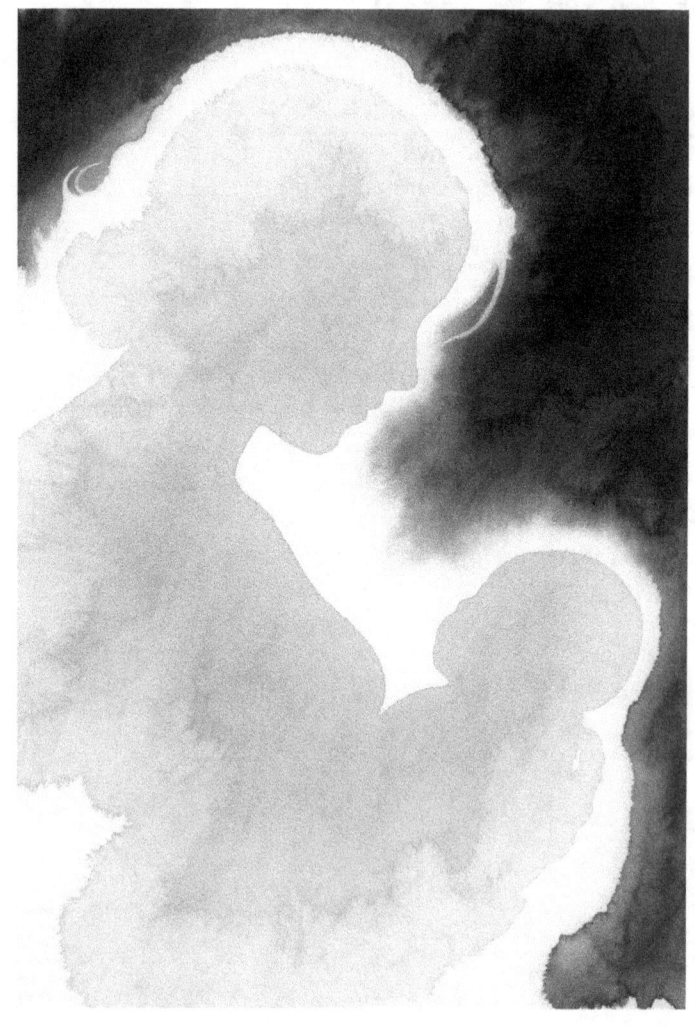

CHAPTER 8

Is It a Boy or Girl?

A child is the hope and the future of
the world, and through their mere
existence, they can heal and save us.

John Lennon

Most airports, even the smaller ones, require a fair amount of walking. This was not optimal for someone who had just had back surgery, so I made my way to our gate via wheelchair. We looked like we were moving across the country with the number of bags we had to check. There were nine to keep track of while traveling: separate suitcases for Nick, the baby, and myself, a stroller, a travel bassinet, a milk box, a car seat, and two backpacks. It seemed like a lot, but most of what was packed would be used at least once. Everything from sterilizing bags for bottle parts, noise machines for sleeping, and every type of outfit from cold to warm was packed since April weather in another state was foreign to us. Anything to reduce our anxiety, we did, since we were not going to be in our own home with the nursery and its supplies at our fingertips.

Other than figuring out how to travel through the airports with all the items on two rolling carts while I was useless in a wheelchair, the traveling went incredibly smoothly. We flew Southwest and were fortunate to get a row where all three of us, Nick, my mom, and myself, could sit together. No luggage was lost, which was my biggest fear. I was incredibly nervous about the milk. We packed a special box to keep breast milk frozen for up to thirty-six hours in transit. We were fortunate to have my cousin's donated breast milk to feed our little one, in addition to whatever Kristi could provide. We wanted to avoid formulas for as long as possible.

We went to Kristi's house as soon as we left the airport. While it was close to 8 p.m. already, we couldn't wait until morning to get a small visit in. The c-section was scheduled for 7:30 a.m. the following day, so we didn't plan to stay too long but had to stop by. We were excited and had to see everyone for a few minutes before the big day. Her kiddos had never met us, and we wanted to say hi to them and make sure they felt supported, too.

Where Kristi and her family lived was nothing short of beautiful. The drive was easy, with no traffic and lots of beautiful country. Granted, the trees were dormant from the winter frost, but being from California, we enjoyed the Illinois beauty. There were almost no streetlights, so we drove slowly to ensure we didn't miss the house. Nick and I love to visit places like this with the humid air, as it is a nice change from our dry California air. It was about sixty-five degrees, and we could smell the fallen leaves in the damp air we breathed.

Her neighborhood was so cute, and the houses all had good-sized lots of an acre or more, it seemed. The backyards were interesting, as we are used to fences, whereas they didn't have fences to separate the yards. I thought it was neat and honestly made the properties look more natural. As we pulled into her driveway, my heart was beating so hard, but in the best way. I was so excited I felt tears swelling, and I couldn't hear anyone or anything for a few seconds.

My nerves eased as soon as one of her sons opened the screen door to let us in. I immediately felt at home and was eager to hug them all. Kristi had the cutest bump, and boy, did she make pregnancy look easy. We all hugged, and then we all teared up, including her husband, Ian. Ian and Nick were so happy to reunite, as they had hit it off before. My mom was immediately welcomed, loved, and fit right in. It felt as if we all had known each other for years. It was strange, but we all loved it. Even the boys were excited.

"You want to see my new Spider-Man?" the youngest asked, not knowing what time it was.

The oldest was more aware and was a little worried about his mom being in the hospital. Kristi and Ian did a great job reassuring him that it would all be okay.

While we all wanted to stay and hang out, we knew we had an early day ahead of us and needed our rest. After mingling and exchanging some of our jitters and excitement with one another, exhaustion hit, and we were ready to try to get at least a few hours of sleep.

I blinked, and the night was gone. Today was the day, and it was very early, 5:30 a.m. We didn't sleep much, but I was full of adrenaline. I couldn't believe we were finally there. God does answer prayers, and it is in His time, which I know is the best time. I was still sore from surgery, but surprisingly, I was doing okay. I confess that I was probably a bit snappy with my mom and loving husband, who tried to help me whenever they could. They knew I had post-surgical limitations, so they did more for me than you would for a typical thirty-four-year-old woman. I didn't want to have restrictions, though, especially then. They were patient with my frustration and stubbornness. I appreciate them and how amazing they have been through all my struggles. God must have known I would need patient family in my life.

We arrived at the hospital bright and early. It wasn't far from the cute little house we had rented. Kristi was the first delivery of the day, so there were no delays. We had very little time to mingle before it was time. We were initially told only one person could be in the room during the delivery.

"The anesthesiologist is nervous about any more people in the room, as it is already a bit crowded in his eyes. I will find a way around it, though; I always do," the OBGYN reassured us confidently.

I didn't want to be in there if it meant Ian couldn't be, as that was his wife. I know Nick would not be comfortable with that if it were me having surgery. After some back and forth, they agreed to let two people be present in the OR. I was still sad because that meant Nick wouldn't be in there. Nick waited in the recovery room across the hall from the delivery room. The doors were clear and not very soundproof, which worked in our favor.

Kristi's husband, Ian, and I needed to gown-up before entering the OR. I quickly put my gown on, and it was *huge*. Ian struggled to even get a leg into his. Ian was much larger than me in both height and build. We were dying laughing as clearly, we had each other's attire by mistake. This relieved us of some of the anxiety we previously suffered with not knowing whether we both would be able to go into the OR. Once dressed, we entered the small OR, or at least it seemed that way with the number of people in there. It was still the most fantastic experience of my life, and I will never forget it.

Ian stayed near his wife's head while I was in full view of where the surgery was performed. Blood, tissue, muscle fibers—none of those things bother me at all. The biology nerd in me came out, and I was fascinated. The nurses, nothing short of amazing, recorded this memory on my phone, allowing me to soak in every bit of our dream come true. I prayed for this; I believed this day would come, but I was terrified of losing it along the way. It seemed too good to be true, but it was simply a blessing and answered prayer.

My hands were over my mouth almost the entire time. I was beside myself with excitement and anticipation. No one knew the sex, so this added to the suspense. As convenient as it is to know the sex, it wasn't something we wanted to focus on. We lost a daughter and all the dreams that came with fantasizing about raising a little girl. We didn't know the feeling of having a son, but we knew it would be exciting in a completely different way.

At 8:13 a.m. on April 5th, the doctor asked, "Well, what is it, Mom?"

With almost no breath, I screeched, "It's a *girl*!" Thankfully, I had enough in me and yelled loud enough for her dad to hear. Kristi and Ian were ecstatic for us. Ian had tears streaming down his face. I can safely say this was the most special out-of-body experience for all of us.

After I cut the umbilical cord, they moved the baby into the recovery room where Nick was. Nick and I watched the nurses take all the measurements and health checks. It was so special. With Paisley, they rushed her off before I could see her, and she had tubes and needles all over her before I was even allowed to walk into the NICU. God bless our sweet girl in Heaven, who we knew was with us on this special day of her baby sister's birth. This newest addition to our family came in, weighing eight pounds and six ounces. How did we get so lucky? God knew we couldn't handle another scare, which was pure bliss.

We already had names picked out for both sexes. If it were to be a boy, we would have named him Ollyver, Olly for short. For a girl, we decided on the beautiful name Jenevieve. Her full name is Jenevieve Paisley Taormina.

While talking to Kristi after she joined us in the recovery room, she asked me, "Do you have a nickname picked out?"

We had come up with a few from this long and elegant name, but the first to come out of my mouth was "Evie." I started to say others like "Jen, Eve, Jenny," but Kristi confirmed, "I like Evie."

"Me, too," I said, and it stuck.

Kristi and I repeatedly hugged and said, "I love you." Ian was there, too; he was as in love with little Evie as we were. It is the weirdest thing when strangers become family almost instantly. We adored and trusted them completely. Nick and Ian may as well have been brothers, as they were two peas in a pod anytime they were in the same room. It flowed, it was natural, it was meant to be. God is good.

After we fed the little chunk some donor milk, she quickly stopped crying. They gave us two ounces to start, and she sucked it down before the nurse could leave.

"I think she's still hungry," I said before the door shut.

The nurse smiled and gladly grabbed another two ounces. Those were sucked down too, and a third helping before she was satisfied for a little while.

The initial room for post-surgery recuperation was temporary, and we were eventually moved to our long-term recovery room in the postpartum area of the hospital. It was beautiful, and the rooms were incredibly spacious and comfortable. They put our room close to Kristi, which was nice. Nick and I stayed with Evie in our room, and my mom stayed most of the day and slept at the rental. My mom was incredibly thoughtful. She brought us, including Kristi and Ian, coffee, snacks, and anything useful for the baby. Everything from the day of Evie's birth was so perfect. I kept waiting for the other shoe to drop, but it didn't.

Everything was as it was supposed to be, and we all felt incredibly blessed.

It is a bit of a sensitive and difficult question to answer when people ask, "Is this your first?" This is our first in many regards, but not our first child. Caring for a NICU baby was different, and our hands were tied in so many ways that made our parenting feel unfairly constrained. However, the privilege of providing milk for my sweet Paisley was the one thing I couldn't do for Evie, so we were beyond blessed to have the donated milk. Initially, I felt guilty that I couldn't breastfeed or pump for Evie. Because we had so much time to process this unique journey and what was to be expected, I accepted our situation and focused on the positives.

We got very little sleep that week in Illinois. We fed every two hours using my cousin's frozen milk. Nick and I switched off feeding and holding every two hours. Sometimes, I stayed awake longer and obsessed over her. We managed to have her burp cloths, diaper-changing necessities, and other miscellaneous items organized in our temporary nursery/bedroom. It wasn't easy living out of suitcases for a week, but we did it, and I was impressed with our novice parental capabilities.

We spent as much time as possible with Kristi and her family and friends, who were all incredibly excited to celebrate the blessed event with us. Evie was loved on by her two boys, Kristi's parents, her close girlfriends, and, of course, Ian and Kristi. Most of the mingling happened over Easter, which was incredibly special. This baby was born so close to such an extraordinary holiday. I believe down to the very last cell in my body that Jesus is the reason Evie is here, and I am, too. I loved how easy this whole visit was. It made me want to stay longer, but I knew we had to get home.

My back was still recovering from surgery, and Nick only had two weeks left before returning to work. After we said the hardest "see you laters" to the family who changed our lives forever, we packed up the rental and prepared for our trip home. We traveled with nine bags and a baby. Thank goodness we had Mom with us to help.

Traveling with a six-day-old infant will get you some looks in an airport. Some were out of concern, while others seemed happy for us. It was an anomaly to many, wondering how a tiny person like me had just given birth. I didn't bother to explain myself unless there was a polite but inquisitive stranger making conversation. Evie was strapped to me while my husband pushed us both in a wheelchair. My back was so grateful.

Once again, Southwest was fantastic. We sat together in the front row with plenty of room. I was relieved to see other babies on the flight, including a sweet nine-month-old, across the aisle. Nick was asleep before takeoff. He was out for the count. Jenevieve was sleepy herself. We all felt relieved knowing this little miracle was coming home, happy and healthy.

I didn't sleep. Miss Jenevieve managed to dirty three diapers during the six-hour flight, filling the trash bags that the flight attendants provided. She ate three times, as anticipated. We used a cordless and waterless electric bottle warmer for these meals, which was the best investment. I highly recommend having one when traveling with an infant without a milk-producing breast. When she wasn't eating or having a diaper change, she focused on the light-up icons above our seats. She was silent, not a peep. We were blessed with a safe trip home.

Our drive home was a little rough, as Jenevieve vocalized her frustration with the travel when we were twenty minutes from home after already being in the car for forty minutes. My bonus dad, Todd, picked us up and helped us gather our seemingly endless bags. He had the extra car seat ready for us, so there was no need to unpack the one we traveled with. He was terrific, and I could tell he was excited, too.

We were pleasantly surprised by our kind neighbors across the way as we pulled up to our driveway. They had covered our porch with beautiful, welcoming decor for our sweet Evie P. So many of our neighbors were beyond excited for us, and we were eager to have them meet Jenevieve. However, that night, we were beat and needed food and sleep. Lots of both. Another neighbor was generous enough to have dinner delivered shortly after we arrived. *Whew, no cooking. Yay!* It was just Nick, Evie, and me for the night. My mom and Todd kept our pups at their place while we settled in.

We had a bassinet next to the bed, although she contact-slept most of the time. On our chests is where she wanted to be, and we were okay with that. I will admit that I was that person who strongly felt that I would never co-sleep, and boy, did I put my foot in my mouth. We ensured no blankets were around her, and a safe flat comforter was underneath me during the night. We knew the risks of SIDS and babies accidentally suffocating themselves, so we were careful and had done enough research to feel comfortable.

Initially, I justified the "why" behind our parenting choices, but that quickly faded, as I knew there were no experts and that we should do what was right for us. On average, Jenevieve slept about 50 percent of the time in her SNOO bassinet, which is like a "smart bassinet" that could rock her side to side with a rhythm dictated by how fussy she was. Don't ask me how this thing worked; I only knew it was our savior many nights. It could securely swaddle her in a breathable sack with Velcro and a zipper while swaying her back and forth to a soothing white noise. We were in survival mode but also a state of peace. I'd been longing for this level of tranquility for what felt like an eternity. I will always miss Paisley Renee, our firstborn, my baby who made me a mama, but Evie helped heal some of the wounds I feared I would live with forever.

Even when Nick returned to work, he took night shifts as Dad once or twice when he could. He was a super-dad. He amazed me and continues to make me so proud. The reality was that I struggled with my health, and it wasn't long before I had issues with my abdomen and digestion once again. The PIC was filling again and needed draining.

Yes, I had to go in for this issue once more, but I was grateful that it was done as an outpatient procedure this time. I was admitted for a couple of days at first, as the doctors needed to find someone who could access the cyst without penetrating the intestinal walls. It was a tricky spot, and we did not want them to open me up again. Fortunately, the interventional radiologists could laparoscopically place a drain into the cyst that I would be responsible for flushing with iodine and draining for a month. I am sure many parents can empathize when I say that the only thing worse than being away from your baby is being hospitalized and at the mercy of those trying to heal you. I felt like a prisoner, even with fantastic physicians and nurses. The experience was all too familiar. Having a NICU baby had instilled trauma I didn't know was there about being forced to sleep miles away from my baby. I experienced this all over again when hospitalized. I was crawling out of my skin.

Once home, the draining became routine for me. My mom also came over every day to help. Jenevieve was not a difficult baby, but I still really needed the support. The draining I had to do twice daily stung like you wouldn't believe. The first week, it was nearly impossible to carry Evie without wanting to scream. It made my entire lower abdomen ache and burn internally like the sting of alcohol poured onto an open wound. That is what the iodine was supposed to do: irritate the inner lining of the PIC to hopefully allow the skin to seal shut after being drained. I hated needing assistance, but I was grateful for my mom.

I struggled throughout this journey with accepting help without feeling guilty. The irony, though, is that I am good at putting myself in the shoes of others, and I love to support others as well. Why was this so dang hard for me? Why was I constantly feeling terrible about my mother's help? When I showed remorse, my mom would remind me of Paisley and me being a mom to her. When my firstborn was in the NICU, I spent all day with her. I pumped, did skin-to-skin, changed diapers, and read every page of the binder they provided for caring for her, all while sitting with intense back pain and no meds for relief. I did everything possible for her; she was my baby, and that's what parents do. I am so lucky to have the mom I do.

"That's what parents do," my mom reaffirmed with tears in her eyes. "We want to."

I knew that I needed to change my outlook on receiving help. After much time, reflection, and growth, I realized that a significant reason for having trouble accepting the selfless acts of others is my perception of my worthiness.

Evie was the light at the end of the long, dark tunnel I was blindly trudging through. Before Paisley, I would fantasize about walking my baby in a stroller alongside my neighbor mamas. I would daydream about baby smiles and my dogs playing with her gently. I envisioned us reading books and rocking to sleep together. Evie helped heal the wounds associated with these desires. While I will always feel I should have had this with my sweet Paisley, I felt gratitude for her being our beautiful guardian angel. In my eyes and faith, I felt there was a piece of her in Evie that would shine through. Paisley picked her out for us, in a sense. There is a good chance that Evie wouldn't be here if the series of events had not happened as they did. She was made in a petri dish with my egg and Nick's sperm. Who knows if meiosis, the random genetic combining of egg and sperm, would have chosen her had she been made the old-fashioned way. In other words, cancer and Paisley both allowed this sweet girl to be created. For that, I am forever grateful.

CHAPTER 9

Some Revisions Need Revising

Keep your face always toward
the sunshine – and shadows
will fall behind you.

Walt Whitman

The first three months flew by, as many of my mom-friends told me they would. Between preparing bottles, changing outfits and diapers, attempting to clean up all the spit up before the dogs got it, feeding our little foodie every two hours, and trying to keep up with the laundry and other household chores, I understood why sleep deprivation was a given with newborns. It was terrific *and* rough. We all become delusional and argue over the most minor things when exhausted, but for Nick and me, this was something we fought so hard for, and we had surprisingly good patience with each other. We were also adjusting to having so much time with each other; weeks in a row were far from ordinary.

From what I've heard, many couples begin to feel the tension of being around one another twenty-four-seven for days or weeks while tending to someone who is utterly dependent on you. It is totally understandable, and I would have assumed we would be this way if our circumstances were typical. Nick and I had spent so much time away from each other, between numerous hospital stays for chemo, surgeries, and two months in Southern California for proton radiation, we were playing catch up on our time together, too. It was a blessing to have this time with each other at home. I had no plans for any more surgeries; I was on the mend…right?

Fast forward to July 2023. Evie was three and a half months old and healthy as can be. She was eating well, and all her checkups went perfectly. I guess her only struggle was baby eczema, but we quickly found effective ways to manage it. Life as a new mom was going well, except for some back pain that had crept its way back into my healing body. It began hurting in mid-June, but I thought I was just sore. With a lack of sleep, being over thirty, and tending to a newborn, I was sure my body hated me to some degree, and this pain was a new norm. I realized, though, as the weeks went by, the agony was getting worse, and it felt familiar. The pain was nearly identical to the discomfort felt back in March with the broken screw. More broken hardware seemed unlikely, as I am a small person, and I wasn't doing anything physical other than caring for a newborn. I had a sharp, excruciating jolt in my lower left sacral area when I took a step with either foot. I tried working on my gait and stretching what I could, hoping for relief. I would bathe, shower, use heating pads, and do everything I could think of that was approved by my surgeons. Nothing helped. I had been there before.

Asking a young woman who just had the best dream come true to go to the ED and leave their newborn at home is insane. Nine times out of ten, when I checked myself in, I didn't come out that same day. This has been my reality since 2021. I was stubborn, as usual, and tried to convince my husband and mom to let me stay home with this pain. Once I began thinking rationally, I realized that it was in everyone's best interest, especially my daughter's, for me to be examined. I now know that this wasn't just me being stubborn, but it was also my medical trauma that made it a battle to accept being admitted into the ED. The pain was where my tumor was, where a screw had broken before, where I had had a fistula and went septic, so not to be concerned and take care of it would be foolish and irresponsible. I had a daughter who depended on me, and I wanted to be dependable. I silenced my stubborn gene and went to the hospital for a scan.

This hospital is far enough from home that my mom insisted on taking me. My back was in no shape to drive the distance and sit in an ED for hours. I always hoped for the best but expected the worst regarding ED visits. The hours of waiting were normal no matter where we went. I learned that at the beginning of the week, around 8 a.m., there was little waiting. I was scheduled for both a CT and MRI scan quickly. This may have been partly due to me informing my neurosurgery team that I was coming as I left my house. It was sad but comforting that the team knew me so well that they were willing to see me in person, even in the ED. The residents working under my surgeon thoroughly checked my reflexes, nerves, and strength throughout my body. Given my history, it was obvious that my being there meant I had an issue. The hospital was the *last* place I wanted to be, with or without a baby at home, and they knew this.

The CT results came back first. Nothing out of the ordinary was seen. That was frustrating. They ordered X-rays as well, and nothing concerning was revealed. The MRI was also okay. My complete blood count didn't show anything abnormal, at least for me. This is where they can assess if I need any blood transfusions or platelets. My baseline for both white blood cell and red blood cell counts had been low since chemotherapy. If I'm being honest, I was secretly hoping one of these counts would be off or the bloodwork would show something abnormal to explain my pain. I was beyond frustrated with no answers from either the blood or scans, as I had been here before. I needed to muster up the strength to advocate for myself.

I will say that in my experience, it is not the fault of the doctors or even the hospital when extreme advocating by the patient becomes necessary; instead, it is more insurance companies that tie their hands. Insurance companies often won't approve of any type of procedure if the scans performed don't reveal convincing enough reasons for them to do so. This is wrong as the surgeons are the professionals, and scans often miss vital information that can only be seen under a knife or through another necessary procedure. I prayed for a long-term solution, no matter how difficult, and that they wouldn't give me pain meds and send me home. I needed more than a band-aid.

Well, my prayer was answered. To our surprise, my surgeon, who had opened me up four times in the back, trusted me and my reasons for being there, and I was admitted. I knew something was broken. Thankfully, I was admitted to the neurosurgery floor, where I would be close to my team. Since this hospital was *always* over capacity with admitted patients, I feared being placed in what we jokingly called a "broom closet." My mom had to sit on my bed when I was admitted into these makeshift rooms because there was no space for even the smallest chair. I also feared being admitted into a shared room because this almost always meant even less sleep than the hospital norm, a shared bathroom, and a higher risk of getting sick. I had been immunocompromised for a couple of years at this point, so I knew my odds of catching something were high. I was blessed this time, as I had my own room on the optimal floor with the care I needed.

With no clear indication from the scans for what could be going wrong, I was anxious to know the plan. I hated being hospitalized with my baby at home. I felt like a prisoner as my motherly instincts told me to pull the lines out of my arm and flee. This was not a realistic solution, and I needed fixing. I was also uneasy because my husband needed to know how much time he had to take off and how many days and nights he would care for Evie alone. Yes, I know some single parents do it, but I didn't want the night feedings and the other care to all fall on him. Night feedings can get to you after a while with no one to relieve you. He also had no more paid days off, which meant we would go without pay. I hoped I would be in and out with a speedy recovery for everyone's sake. Unfortunately, the solution to my pain was not that simple.

I was told I would need another back surgery. A "revision."

"What does that entail?" I asked the neurosurgery team with concern.

I also inquired about what would happen if nothing was found once opened. Would they just sew me back up and have me recover? Would they replace anything? What would be the next steps? My mind was spinning, as I did not want to undergo another surgery with any possibility of nothing being fixed. I was incredibly nervous now as I contemplated whether to go through with the procedure. I prayed and slept on it and decided that the potential risks outweighed the current pain I was in. I had faith that something was wrong and they would find it.

I was hospitalized for two days before the day of my surgery. Without knowing precisely what would be done, there was no telling how long I would be there. I had already had multiple twelve-hour surgeries, so I knew I could handle whatever this procedure threw my way. My surgery was about seven hours long, and yes, they found the problem. The screw that was replaced in February was broken *again*. No one wishes to have broken hardware in their bodies, but when there is intense pain that shows up daily with no relief, you wish for a fixable problem to show itself. Rather than replace the broken screw using the same method as the previous surgery, my surgeon did a bit more. He not only replaced the screw but added another screw and an additional rod. The hardware on the left side of my spine had been replaced entirely. Originally there were three screws and one rod on the left and four screws and one rod on the right, all made from a metalloid called molybdenum rhenium. With the repeatedly failed screw, the surgeon decided that all hardware on the left side should be replaced with a thicker gauge titanium. To summarize this revision, I had all the hardware to the left of my spine removed and replaced, resulting in two titanium rods and four titanium screws, all while the metalloid rod and screws to the right were left alone. I was closed with a total of eight screws and three rods.

I was frustrated and relieved at the same time. I was upset that the same screw broke, as this gave me little to no confidence in the future of this new screw, let alone the rest of the hardware. My surgeon did an excellent job reassuring me that what was done should hold better than the last setup. He told me I was a "one in a million" case. This is not a compliment but more a scary reality. I came to accept that I was, give-or-take, an experimental case. It's not their fault I was at their mercy, but I was sad, scared, and flat-out angry. I had to begin my recovery all over again, meaning that I couldn't bend, lift, or twist for another year. I had a baby to care for, yet I was to recover and rest from a significant and unexpected back surgery.

I hoped for a speedy recovery and to be home as soon as possible. Unfortunately, some post-surgical complications came as a surprise to not only me but the neurosurgery team as well. I couldn't feel my entire pelvic floor; none of my privates had any sensation, nor did they have control. I had what they call "saddle anesthesia." I had many accidents as I couldn't control my anal sphincter muscles whatsoever. I was worried, and so was the team. They ordered STAT MRI and CT scans to ensure a nerve wasn't severed or pinched, causing this issue. Nothing was found on the scans, leading them to believe that the only cause for this could be the spinal fluid leak, which was an unexpected complication during this last surgery. During the surgery, the dura that holds the fluid surrounding the spine and nerves tore slightly. This is not too uncommon, especially for someone like me, with a ton of scar tissue from past operations. I was not concerned about that, as the dura, fortunately, repaired itself during the first recovery day. The pelvic floor nerves, however, were numb for the entire time I was in recovery. Nerves are tricky, as they take a long time to repair. I was told we had to wait and see if the saddle anesthesia would improve. This was frustrating, as I had to live in diapers until further notice. While this situation was a grave concern to me, I was more adamant about getting home to change my baby's diapers rather than my own. I was given the green light to go home after a week and a half of in-patient recovery.

My doctor recommended that I have at least a month of full-time help when I was discharged. I needed to wear my back brace full time, and I was not to lift anything over five pounds, even my baby, when possible. I was beyond excited to see Evie. I could hardly stand it. The thought of holding her again had my eyes swelling with tears on the ride home. I needed to be near, smell, hug, feed, and be her mom.

I cried like a baby and trembled when the front door slowly opened as my mom and I walked up the driveway. Both my husband and father-in-law, Steve, stood in the doorway with the largest smiles. My father-in-law recorded the special moment of reunion, and I was so grateful, as the moment was almost surreal and a blur. Evie, only four months old then, was happy too but blissfully unaware of what was happening. I hugged Nick and Evie while he held her. It felt so good, like when I held Paisley after being away from her all night. The roles were reversed with Evie, as I was the sick one and hospitalized while she was healthy and at home. In both scenarios, a mom and child were separated. I couldn't wait to sit and have Evie on my lap.

Being away from your baby is never easy. Not having a child to care for when you are a mom can cause an empty feeling. When Evie came, it felt like I had pushed the resume button on parenthood but was forced to click pause again with the failed hardware. I continued to blame not only my body but also the hardware company. I pushed my anger and frustration aside. I was blessed to be home with my family. My father-in-law was terrific, and I appreciated his help during this difficult time. Nick had his dad spend most nights while I was gone, and they both got bonding time together, and Papa got to spend quality time with his newest granddaughter. Silver linings are essential, and I tried hard to look for them during the dark times. With their help, my mom was able to be with me in the hospital. Otherwise, she would have stayed to help care for Evie. They say it takes a village, and whoever *they* are, they are right. That evening, my mom, Nick, father-in-law, Evie, and I enjoyed each other's company. We even heard Evie's giggle, the icing on the cake.

During my hospitalization, my mom was also caring for her dad. My ninety-four-year-old grandpa was staying in her home. He had dementia and needed full-time care. I felt so guilty and pushed my mom away, hoping she would prioritize him over me. I was a long drive away, and I knew how much he needed her to stay. My mom, the strongest woman I know and full of wisdom, explained that being a mom came first, always. It wasn't hard for me to put myself in her shoes, as nothing would ever come before caring for either of my babies. Her husband and my bonus dad, Todd graciously stepped in to help with the care of my grandfather. It wasn't easy, but I knew he wanted to and was happy to do it. I felt the love from everyone but often allowed myself to bear guilt rather than gratitude. I'd needed help for too many years; frankly, I was sick of it. I would often go into my stubborn, angry worlds and want to push everyone away, not because I didn't care for and appreciate them, but because I loved them so much and wanted more for my family and friends. I felt like a burden. I assume my grandfather felt the same. He was ninety-four, though, and I was thirty-four, a big difference. It's safe to say that a mother in her thirties would never plan to wear and go through more diapers than her four-month-old baby.

I said I was done for the last two-and-a-half years. I felt like this time, though, I couldn't say it because I genuinely knew I wasn't. Jenevieve was saving me by giving me purpose. I had a piece of my identity back, and it felt good. Being a mom looked different than I had imagined, but I was grateful. She didn't care that I wore diapers, so I tried not to. It was hard, though. I had accidents throughout the day and at least two at night. For better or for worse, it became routine.

Unfortunately, saddle anesthesia wasn't something that could simply be reversed or cured in any way; it was something that would need to be fixed, and only time would tell how. The last thing I wanted was an accident outside my home, where there may or may not be an ideal opportunity to change and clean myself up. If there were ever a reason for me to get anxious, it would be about this. For almost three years, I had been recovering either in a hospital or at home, too fragile to go out and socialize. Oh, and COVID caused us all to have cabin fever before all this. I was tired of having to say no to outings.

Despite not knowing when I would need to deal with my diaper situation, I still tried to do what I felt was good for me. I went on walks, sometimes having to quickly return home, change, and go back out if Evie was okay with it. Some days, I let my health defeat me, and that's valid, too. I genuinely believe there will be days when we face and process the music head-on. I don't usually sit in my situation all day, but give myself a moment. I talk to my mom or Nick about where I am emotionally and then move on. The frustration doesn't usually last too long if you have good people in your life who can remind you of how well you are doing. Sometimes, it is impossible to be proud of myself. Maybe it's because I am too close to it.

CHAPTER 10

Two Steps Forward, One Step Back...

Out of suffering have emerged the strongest souls; the most massive characters are seared with scars.

Khalil Gibran

It was now December of 2023, a month filled with gratitude and sadness, at least in this house. I don't think I am alone in these feelings, as the holidays can remind us of those we wish were with us. It makes sense, as this is usually the season for families to get together, exchange gifts, make memories, and eat lots of good food. Many follow traditions passed down or created in new homes with growing families. When we moved into our new home in 2020, we were eager to make our own Christmas traditions. However, we had no idea that each December from then until now would be so different.

Change is often stressful, but this year, it was the best thing that could have happened to our healing hearts. Evie's new presence lit up every room with the most contagious smile, showing off all six teeth. At eight months old, she had a toy playpen where she could self-entertain and learn a lot with some new independence. She was crawling and rolling by this time, so the pen helped Mom and Dad know she was staying out of trouble. She loved all cords, whether plugged in or not and when she was "free," she would roll or crawl at high speed, making a beeline for the very thing she wasn't supposed to have. She was never left unsupervised, especially since she decided movement was pretty dang cool once she mastered it. This age was an incredible time as I watched the wheels constantly turning in her beautiful, growing mind. It was change that was healing.

My heart explodes with genuine gratitude for our sweet Evie. However, I couldn't help but wonder what it would have been like to have an almost three-year-old experiencing the Christmas season with her baby sister. Dreams will always be there, and sometimes they can creep to the surface, especially when making memories becomes intentional. Sometimes, I would wish for Christmas time, followed by New Year's Eve, which is Paisley's birthday, and then the day of her passing on January 9th to be over. I wanted the hard days gone. There were mixed feelings this past year, as I also wanted to take in and appreciate the memories of Evie during her first holiday season. Grief is like a wound that never fully heals. We get better at bandaging it with time. From what many have told me, I am handling the cards we've been dealt well.

I can't look at Evie without feeling like the luckiest mom in the whole world. She is perfect. She deserves the world and the best mama. I wanted to be the mom I dreamed I would be, but I was struggling physically. The saddle anesthesia continued to handicap me into wearing diapers full-time. Even though the diapers came with anxiety when leaving the house, I was determined to get out and do something special on January 9th to honor our sweet Paisley's passing. We took Evie to the aquarium for the first time, and she loved it. Everything from the jellyfish to the penguins had her wholly captivated. This was the dream. Well, almost. The struggle with diapers didn't stop. With no food in my system, I still managed to have three accidents that required me to interrupt our family time to find the closest restroom. It was the straw that broke the camel's back. The diaper changing, with frequent and unexpected accidents, needed to stop. I was done, as it was dramatically affecting my quality of life. I needed a more permanent and manageable solution.

The following week, I contacted my general oncology surgeon, who had previously placed my temporary ostomies in the past. After speaking with him and some GI specialists, they agreed that the best solution for my case would be to place yet another ostomy, my third one, with no intention of taking it out in the future. It would be forever this time, assuming that the saddle anesthesia was also here to stay. I never thought the day would come when I would request such a thing. I hated them in the past and counted down the days until they would be gone. I mentally prepared for this stoma, the part of the intestine that would protrude through my abdomen that would be here to stay. I had to learn to adapt yet again.

I seem to be okay when my surgeries are scheduled or somewhat planned. I have a level head and focus on the benefits I pray will come from them. Due to a crazy healthcare system, I was instructed to go to the ED for my saddle anesthesia, as my surgeon could get me in for surgery sooner than if I was scheduled. This might sound wild to some, but it made sense to me with my experience in waiting for an OR. We made sure to go in on a Monday, as we knew we had an entire week with my surgeon on staff. Unfortunately, that upcoming Monday was a holiday, so the ED was busier than usual.

I will spare you the ED wait and chaos, as it was nothing out of the norm. Once I was seen, to our surprise, even with the hospital extremely full, I got into a room without a roommate. Yes, a room on the floor my surgeon works on regularly! This was a massive win for me, as I knew recovering from this surgery would be challenging, and privacy was paramount. It's safe to assume that no one wants to be in pain with a roommate. Once I was settled into my room, I quickly found out that my surgery was tentatively scheduled for the next day. God was looking out, as I had the most challenging time being away from my sweet girl. I wanted to get in and out so I could be home.

I hoped that this surgery could be done laparoscopically, but I was assured that was not an option. After so many surgeries, this would be the seventh time they would open me up vertically down my abdomen. With scar tissue everywhere, muscles and organs moved around multiple times, bones missing, and hardware placed in various locations, the surgeons needed to have a better and more open visual. This was fine, I guess, but I was discouraged, as I knew the recovery would take longer. I was all about healing fast and getting home to my Evie P.

Before the surgery, I met with some ostomy nurses who helped mark the most optimal location for the stoma's placement. This also meant that the collection bag would be placed there, so you wanted it to be in the most convenient spot, if there is such a thing. With a short torso and scars from previous ostomies in the lower left abdominal region, this left us with few options. We cannot go over the scars, but I tried to prevent the ostomy from being right under the ribcage, where it would become a nuisance every time I bent over. We decided that the lower right side would be the best first option, and the least favorable place would be under the ribs on the left side. I had three marks for the surgeon to choose from during the surgery.

While I was told where the best place for the stoma would be, the nurse didn't realize I was missing abdominal muscles on the right side, so that area wound up being completely off-limits. The surgeon himself informed me that it had to be placed under the ribs on the left side, which I quickly learned to be okay with. At least I had already been in the habit of carrying Evie on my right hip. Small wins are what I focused on. Another positive was that she would have a mama who could manage her waste output more efficiently than diapers, and she could still be held. *Let's do this!*

After the ostomy surgery, I was sore, but I was prepared for it. I know every surgery is different, even if you've had one similar before. The seventh time slicing through the same scar meant the scar tissue and healthy skin had to heal again. The human body is fantastic, but it still takes time. I was up and walking right away and was only bothered by the severe gas pains. Don't get me wrong, I was on strong pain medications for a few days, but I quickly got off them, thinking this could get me home sooner. I thought Friday was going to be the day, but I had some unexpected pain arise the night before. I was glad it happened before being discharged. I learned my lesson in August about going home before I was ready. It is so much more complicated when you are a mom, as your brain almost tricks you into thinking you are physically okay and healed when you aren't so you can care for your babies. It's a blessing and a curse because I needed to recover to care for her long-term, so I had to take a step back and be patient as a patient. Luckily, my father-in-law Steve stayed at our home to support his son however he could, all while enjoying time as Papa. There are always silver linings to these problematic events, one being that Nick, his dad, and Evie all got some quality time that is not easy to come by. I like to look at my surgeries as blessings, as they gave Nick the chance to have more time at home than most working parents often get.

I would love to say that a third ostomy meant my acceptance of one would be easier, but that is far from the truth, or at least it was for me. I knew the freedoms of this lifestyle would be preferable to the hundreds of diapers I went through. Still, I'd never been forced to have the mindset of it being permanent. The ones in the past were strictly placed to allow the lower lumbar flaps placed by plastics to recover post-surgery, so I always had a date for when it would be reversed.

I thought I was doing well until I got home and made a rookie move. I emptied my bag into the toilet and forgot to close the bottom of the bag. *Who does that? I mean, come on!* I'd had these before and didn't remember making this mistake. I got my Ugg slippers all messed up, and I cried. It wasn't about the slippers, even though they *were* my good ones. It was about the fact that I couldn't say, "This will end soon." Rather than count down the weeks for motivation, I reminded myself that tomorrow was a new day, and I would have some days that didn't go as planned. It shouldn't come as a surprise to anyone that several things can go wrong with ostomy bags. I mean, our babies have blowouts, while some of us have leaking bags. Oh well, it happens. I won't speak for others who have one, but I have a list of struggles that I've experienced with my ostomies. Not only has the bag broken open while sleeping and accidentally rolling on it, but I've had the ring seal adhered to the skin break loose and leakage come from there. I've left the bag open and made a mess, and several times, I struggled in so many ways while changing the bag to a new one. In my opinion, they are not an easy lifestyle change to implement.

In the short time since the surgery, I had more meltdowns than I'd like to admit. A few were alone, but most were in my mom's or Nick's arms. I hated the guilt that came with these moments, as I felt like the most enormous imposition after my tears were dried. I am the first to admit that I haven't always handled these complex changes with ideal grace over the last three years. It felt as if my primitive fight-or-flight responses to what I was feeling were in complete control. I was selfish at these times, but I am learning that it was also me trying to survive. Of course, I discovered later that the support from those who love me so much was what I needed, and they were happy to do it.

When I was overwhelmed, though, and the world felt as if it was caving in, I would self-sabotage and push my husband away when, deep down, I knew I needed him the most. The man who, without question, would come in to clean up my mess after my stoma leaked all over the floor. You know you've found your person when they are happy to help you clean up your literal "crap." No matter how difficult your journey might be, do not push those who choose to be there for you and with you away. Let them help. Trust me, I have plenty of experience.

Silly things get to me now that didn't before. I have a petite frame, so this stupid bag is evident. "It's not a tumor," as Arnold Schwarzenegger said in *Kindergarten Cop*, always comes to mind when I wonder what others might be thinking about the giant awkward-looking bump under my shirt. My clothes, which I once thought were cute, no longer felt cute. I never cared too much about my appearance at home with Evie. Still, if I had to go out or felt like wearing "real clothes" (as opposed to my usual loungewear), I allowed myself to break down. It felt petty, as it's not the end of the world for me to have a tummy bulge. Again, the tears stemmed from the fact that it was one more thing to struggle with for life. Change is a stressor, and I was stressed. It's been hard to accept every physical change I've had to adapt to over such a short time.

As adults, we learn that life will always throw pressure at us. Always. It was pointless to wait for that opportunity for the strains we inevitably must face to stop landing on our doorstep before we decide to live our lives. If you're waiting for everything to get easier before you breathe, *stop*. You will die of suffocation, I promise you. This next chapter will explain how what I once thought was happening *to* me was, in fact, happening *for* me.

CHAPTER 11

Gratitude

Sometimes the hardest storms
bring the most beautiful rainbows.
Our greatest blessings often
come disguised as challenges,
for it is through adversity that we
uncover strength, resilience, and
silver linings that would never have
existed without the struggle.

Alysia Taormina

Every moment, even those that almost kill us emotionally, spiritually, or physically, presents us with opportunities for gratitude. These experiences present the most valuable silver linings we must appreciate and hold onto for life. Everyone has their definition of a silver lining. For me, silver linings are the blessings that shine through the struggles and adversity we face in life. I am sure I don't see them all, and I may have often turned a blind eye to them when they made themselves present in the past. The beauty of these silver linings is that they have patience. They stay. They wait for you to notice them in your own time. They are holy blessings from the God I know and love. The hard pill to swallow is that you must endure difficult experiences or sometimes watch others you love go through them to see some of these blessings. I don't believe everyone has to endure *your* struggles to see, feel, and benefit from the silver linings that arise if you are brave enough to share them with the world.

I have heard so many times that God works through broken people, but the thing is, we are all broken. Ironically, we are all struggling in our own ways, yet we compare. This is unfortunate, as comparison robs us of our potential happiness. We compete with the lives of others, including possessions, where we feel we should be in life, even where we are regarding our mission with God (if you are a believer). During these last few years, the number one comparison I continuously made was not to others but to my past. I wanted badly to have all that I had lost and was not ready to let go of what was and focus on what is. I was so fixated on what was taken and wasn't thinking about what I had gained. I won't say I never envied others, as I most certainly did. I was envious of anyone who could get pregnant at their leisure, use any piece of gym equipment to strengthen their healthy body, or jog when under immense stress, and anyone not at the mercy of a hospital, day in and day out. I felt like a prisoner of my illness, and it often sent me down the path of dwelling on what it had taken from me. With time, I learned a lot about what was gained, and I felt foolish for taking as long as I did to see all the beautiful blessings robbed by my choice to compare.

Some of the lessons I learned were not easy, nor were they seen as blessings in the beginning. When the adversities of child loss and cancer arose, I unknowingly had expectations of others, predominantly close family. I will spare you the drama; we all have enough in our relationships. I learned that not everyone we depend on will be there for us in the ways we need, but many you didn't expect will step up and fill those voids. Blood is not always thicker than water, and our chosen family can often become more valuable than our family of origin. The support I received and continue to have poured into me and my family comes from those I *choose* to have in my life. I learned that we should not have expectations of anyone, even if they are the closest blood family member. Expectations can be tricky, as I do believe it is okay to have them within reason of those you love and value in your life. In my experience, I have discovered that what is considered "reasonable" is a matter of perspective and priorities. Based on their actions, we can choose whether their priorities fit into our lives in ways that make sense at that time. I also discovered that people sometimes have seasons; not all friends and family will be in our lives forever.

I can confidently say that my mindset and priorities are nowhere near where I imagined they would be in my mid-thirties. A silver lining I'm grateful for, though, is my way of looking at life. The lenses I get to look through are unique and help me admire life in a light that not all can see or understand. This is not to sound pretentious or boastful. It's the forced perception of what's important to someone who has walked in my shoes. While the loss of relationships and distance from family members are sad, I realized over the last couple of years that it's also okay and usually what's best for everyone. I've heard many say that it took them well into their fifties or sixties before they realized the importance of not forcing unhealthy relationships on themselves and their family. It goes both ways, so I am not saying that those we've distanced ourselves from were bad people, and we are, in fact, perfect. If you're not fitting into our lives well, we are probably unsuitable for yours. It's that simple, and I like to keep it that way.

I genuinely empathize with mamas who must leave their babies for any length of time, but even more so for those with babies being hospitalized. Leaving Paisley at the NICU for the first time was what I thought would be the most harrowing night of my life. Unfortunately, eight nights later would be the most devastating, as it was our last. You might ask yourself where the silver lining would be in this scenario. I did for a long time, too. It took three years and becoming a mom to another baby to see it, if I'm being honest. The rose-colored glasses I get to look through while raising Jenevieve are made up of tears, heartbreak, and NICU memories and trauma. They are priceless. It sounds weird, but let me explain. I can't look at Jenevieve and her beautiful life without feeling an explosion of gratitude. She's under our roof every dang night. Her baths are in a tub in her own home. She is growing and healthy while living the dream I had for her, and oh my goodness, I know how amazing that is. Every child is a blessing, which is well known, but when you lose one, I genuinely believe you will be forever changed. I hope that these silver linings I continue to share can help you through the grief, struggles, and trauma that may be experienced and cannot be forgotten. I truly believe you cannot see the bright blessings without acknowledging the dark parts of your life that brought them to fruition.

I imagine we all have some rose-colored glasses to look through; some might not be worn as often, or maybe accepting difficult memories causes us to keep seeing the world through these lenses. Timing is everything, and these lenses and the silver linings they expose will be waiting for the right time. My novice advice would be not to wait too long, as time is precious, and our memories should be as beautiful as possible.

Where were the silver linings in me becoming ill and needing chemotherapy, IVF, radiation, and several surgeries? All cancer did was give me losses: my health, ability to carry a child, hair, muscle, bone structure, ability to exercise, ability to walk without a limp, normal intestinal functions, my ability to teach, time with my family, and more. What did I gain? "Nothing." This was my mindset for a good long while. Every day, usually in a hospital, I would wake up feeling this way. It went from every day to every other day to every few days. My mind and heart began to strengthen, and I eventually only had moments within a day of feeling these things. I need to share this to allow anyone in a dark place to realize that it's okay and that I have been there. I'm not going to lie and tell you all my losses came back in the end and that this will be the same for you. I will share that my losses are only significant because of what they allowed me to gain. While my health remains questionable and my body has seen better days, I have been able to spend every day and night (minus the ones taken by some unexpected surgeries) with my sweet Evie! I *never* thought that was in the cards for me! I love teaching, and I loved the idea of having every afternoon and evening with my family, but I get even more now! This may sound unbelievable to some, but spending time with Evie and my family makes the challenges of my health journey completely worth it!

The most significant and most well-hidden silver lining was the loss of Paisley. How would I find a silver lining in that tragic and traumatic experience? I believe God revealed these blessings to me in His time, which was not right away. After she passed, I, of course, couldn't make sense of it and truly felt that nothing good would ever come of it. It turns out that this little warrior brought many powerful silver linings to us when she went to Heaven. Acknowledging these blessings by no means implies that I am glad she is gone. It is meant to reveal her importance, highlight her strength, and show how proud we are to be her parents. To start, Paisley's life gave me the fantastic experience of being pregnant, becoming a mom, and loving another life unconditionally. She also taught me how to fight and be brave. Paisley's arrival at thirty weeks gestation is what kept my tumor from having more time to grow, break, and quickly spread. The reality is that my cancer was found in time because of her. She saved my life. Had she lived through my cancer journey, I may have made some choices that would have shortened my time here, my time with her, my time as a mom, a wife, and a daughter. I would likely have declined as much treatment as I could simply to be home with her, and treatment may not have even been an option had the cancer spread. Regardless, my priorities would have been different, and that is just me being honest as a mom. Evie is also here because of her brave big sister in Heaven. I know that demanding IVF before beginning chemo most likely wouldn't have been at the forefront of my mind if I hadn't just lost my baby. Jenevieve was brought into this world because of her sister, who opened my mama heart, and there was no going back.

Gratitude is commonly understood as feeling thankful for the good things in our lives. But how deep does that thankfulness run? I believe we can measure our gratitude for each blessing on a scale that shifts daily, monthly, and yearly. What if the very experience of cultivating gratitude is a silver lining in itself? While we can certainly appreciate what we have, facing adversities offers us a unique opportunity to deepen our gratitude.

Nearly four years after Paisley's passing, I find myself grateful for the person I have become through my experiences. I once felt burdened by guilt for not living up to the expectations of others, both physically and mentally. It's difficult to accept that I will never carry another child, that I will always need accommodations for my colostomy bag, and that my sacral and spinal hardware will impose limitations on my activities. Mentally, I face struggles that affect my loved ones as I've changed, and I constantly wrestle with insecurities about my appearance and how to embrace my new body. At times, I still question my worth.

As I come to the end of writing this book, I embrace my true self unapologetically. I've been blessed with a silver lining: the ability to appreciate who I've become through all I've faced. If I tried to revert to the person I felt others wanted me to be, perhaps the version of myself before I lost a child and became ill, I wouldn't have developed this deep sense of gratitude, and this book might never have come to be. It is a story worth sharing, one that embodies hope, faith, and gratitude, all by being unapologetically me.